The Derbyshire "Kraut"

I specially dedicate this book to

Irene and John

Nancy and Wilfried

Jean and Ian

as well as to all our British friends

without their great support

our foreign adventure could have turned

out completely different

Johannes M. Ludwig

THE DERBYSHIRE

"KRAUT"

AN INSPIRING AND MOTIVATING TRUE STORY

Bibliografische Information der Deutschen Nationalbibliothek
Die Deutsche Nationalbibliothek verzeichnet diese Publikation in der Deutschen Nationalbibliografie; detaillierte bibliografische Daten sind im Internet über http://dnb.d-nb.de abrufbar.

Original title: Mut zum Risiko - Vier Jahre Großbritannien
Translated from the original German by: Johannes M. Ludwig
English Proofreading Service: Wissenschaftslektorat Kelly GmbH

Verlag: BoD · Books on Demand GmbH, In de Tarpen 42, 22848 Norderstedt, bod@bod.de
Druck: Libri Plureos GmbH, Friedensallee 273, 22763 Hamburg

ISBN: 978-3-7693-4859-0

TABLE OF CONTENTS

PREFACE

Many years ago, my wife and I lived and worked in the United Kingdom for four years. Although I wrote down the challenges and experiences of this exciting time of unlimited freedom, I subsequently set these notes aside. After an active professional life, the idea of digitizing and publishing these formative memories matured.

The technical tools for planning and realising such a venture have certainly changed in the meantime and, as of January 31, 2020, the UK is no longer a member of the European Union. However, the way we carried out such a project in a foreign country with a great deal of courage and initiative can still inspire others today.

We were very lucky. However, without taking some risks, we would never have encountered this luck. We still have a very special relationship with our former host country, marvellous friends, and unique memories. All of this is priceless. If I could repeat a part of my life, I would choose these four years without hesitation. Although we would certainly be better off financially today if we had started our professional careers in our own country, we would not have been able to gain all these valuable and formative experiences, and some very important people would be missing among our friends.

While editing the text, the memories came flooding back with such intensity as if I had only just left Britain.

Southern Germany, spring 2025
Johannes M. Ludwig

DEPARTURE FROM OSNABRÜCK TO DERBY IN GREAT BRITAIN

Sunday, March 10, 1985. We go for a walk in the old town of Osnabrück - the sun is shining and the weather is mild. An ordinary Sunday afternoon, you might think, in which you recover to be fit for the challenges of a new week. However, for my wife Marie and me, this Sunday afternoon is not like any other, but very special. Today is not only my last day in Osnabrück but also my last day in Germany.

In a few hours, I shall set out on an adventurous journey. The destination is Great Britain. I intend to gain a foothold there during the next few weeks, which means that I will try to find a job and a flat. For the time being, I will be going alone, and my wife will stay in Osnabrück for a while. Only if my search were to be successful will she follow. We want to live and work in the United Kingdom for at least two years, improve our language skills, and gain international experience.

We plan to embark on this foreign adventure completely independently. Will we succeed? In any case, there is no lack of courage and ambition. The decision to realize such a project was made three months ago. We made it together. Now the time has come to implement the ambitious plan.

We return to our flat. Although something extraordinary is about to happen, I'm not nervous. The last time I was in the UK was eleven years ago, and a lot will have changed in the meantime.

My destination is Derby, the English twin town of Osnabrück. While the East Midlands is completely unknown to me, I can stay with a host family for three weeks as the Derby Envoy (the representative of the City of Derby in Osnabrück) was able to arrange that. But, I have to take care of finding a job myself.

Twenty minutes until departure. What awaits me? It's like walking into a pitch-dark room and having no idea what's behind the door.

Then, it's time to say goodbye and leave. If everything goes well, I'll see Marie again in seven weeks. By then, I hope to have found both a job and a flat as only when this is done will she quit her current job and join me abroad. In seven weeks, according to the plan, I want to return to Osnabrück for a few days, help with the packing, and fetch our car. But, until then, much still needs to be done.

One last kiss, one last look back. There is still time to stop the entire project, not to risk anything and carry on as before. But I won't back down! We have carefully planned and prepared everything, and this is how it is now being carried out. Marie smiles at me, and then the front door closes. The journey into the future has just begun, the moment of separation is over, and the whole wide world lies ahead of me.

From the bus stop, I can see Marie standing at the window. She waves at me. Then the bus arrives, I get on, and the journey begins. From the railway station, I want to take the train to Hook of Holland. From there, a ferry will take me to Harwich.

The train leaves the station and passes familiar streets, houses, and landscapes. A feeling of melancholy arises; I pull myself together and think of the adventure that awaits me.

We soon leave familiar territory, and I pick up a book and start reading. At the moment, I just want to be left alone and don't feel like talking to other travellers in the fully occupied compartment. A book in front of one's face is always the best protection to avoid unwanted conversation. Two Englishmen are sitting directly opposite me, talking quietly. The compartment gradually empties, and we approach the Dutch border.

Once we cross the border, only the two Englishmen and I remain in the compartment. The two speak louder now, while I still hide behind my book even though I am no longer reading. Strange! I am going to Great Britain to improve my language skills, want to get to know the country and its people, am sitting across from two Englishmen, and I'm trying to delay striking up a conversation. This is certainly due to the reluctance to take the first step and actively use a foreign language.

The two look over at me from time to time but don't speak to me. After a while, they look over more often, and I'm sure they would like to ask me something. As time passes, I find it ridiculous to keep holding a book in front of me that I do not read any more, pull myself together, and put the literature aside.

Now there is no barrier between me and the other two travellers. We look at each other. A friendly nod, an encouraging smile. One of the two asks me where the journey is going. "To Derby, visiting friends," I reply. Well then, the first step has been taken. The other one wants to know how long I intend to stay. Am I supposed to tell the truth now? Would this perhaps trigger a discussion about the sense (or the lack thereof) of such a project? How would they react? Would they shower me with suggestions regarding my plans, or maybe even advise me against it? The situation in the British labour market is not exactly promising at the moment, it is certainly difficult to find a job. I choose an evasive approach. "I'm going on vacation for three weeks," I reply, and both of them are satisfied. They now show me gifts that they bought for friends and relatives, pulling bottles of wine and liquor, as well as tasty sausages out of their bags. A lively conversation ensues. I don't even notice that I have long since stopped using my native language and adopted that of my host country.

It is dark outside, and the glow of street lamps accompanies the train's journey. During the conversation, I even forgot the time, and now everything suddenly happens very quickly. "Where are we actually?" "Not far from the coast."

We are approaching the Hoek of Holland. I feel good, the first test has been passed successfully. I communicate with English people in their language and understand them. This gives me the boost I so desperately need right now.

We reach the Hoek of Holland, the terminus of the train. From here, the journey continues by ship. My two travel companions are not here for the first time, they know their way around. I follow them. We leave the train station and enter the port area to the ferry that is going in the direction of Great Britain, where all the other travellers also want to go. I follow them and enter a big hall. There is a lot of hustle and bustle. Pieces of luggage lie around everywhere, customs officers control the travellers, passports are checked, and announcements in Flemish and English can be heard from loudspeakers.

It is now 11 p.m. The ferry is scheduled to depart around midnight. I get through customs without any problems, don't even have to open my luggage, exit the port building and – for the first time – see the ferry that will take me across the English Channel tonight. What an impressive sight! In front of me, the huge ship looms brightly lit against the dark night sky. On board, I encounter uniforms, portholes, narrow corridors, and international languages. A reserved berth is waiting for me in a cabin so that I can start the first day in my new host country well-rested. A steward tells me the cabin number and describes how to get there. I descend several stairs that lead deep into the interior of the ferry. There are four of us in the cabin.

After my few belongings are stowed away, I return to the deck. Suddenly I don't feel tired anymore, on the contrary, I feel like exploring the ship. The corridors and halls begin to fill up. In some rooms, there is a pleasant smell of food, in others more of alcohol. Many of the young passengers settle on steps, floors, and lounges to spend the night. I am pleased to have a berth in a cabin where I can sleep more comfortably than on the floor.

Before returning to my cabin, I go on deck for a breath of fresh air, which is very pleasant after the stuffy air inside the ferry. I'm standing at the railing and it's almost midnight. Numerous lights illuminate the opposite side of the harbour. The area in which no lights can be seen and the pitch-black night awaits us must be the open sea. I stay out here for a while, enjoying the calm.

As I stand at the railing and look out over the dark water, my thoughts wander back to Osnabrück, to my wife, who stayed behind there. Not only land but also water will separate us tomorrow. Suddenly, I see what I have left. However, in such a moment of weakness, one should not get sentimental but have to be very clear about having made the right decision, which now has to be implemented.

I suppress the melancholy and look firmly and resolutely to the future. I'll be in the UK tomorrow and will start looking for a job and a place to live. A few months later, Marie will follow. I'm not thinking any further than this at the moment. Time will tell.

It's past midnight and the ship's engines are running - it will depart soon. In a little while, the huge ferry slowly casts off from the pier. The engines roar louder and we glide gently out into the darkness towards the open sea. Harwich will be reached in eight hours. I look into the night towards the sea. Somewhere out there lies Great Britain, and Derby, the destination of my journey. All the people who are still unknown to me live there, whom I shall get to know during the next few years. At this moment, I am full of confidence and feel strong. Let's tackle it, let's experience this adventure.

Suddenly, I feel a pleasant tiredness. One last look out at the dark sea, at the spray generated by our ship, which is now picking up speed, before I return to my cabin deep inside the ferry. The other passengers are already in their bunks and it doesn't take long for me to fall asleep as well.

I wake up in the middle of the night. It's warm and stuffy in the cramped cabin. The faint sound of falling raindrops can clearly be heard, which is impossible because I'm down here deep inside the ship. But, you can hear it clearly. It must be raining outside. This phenomenon is certainly caused by a ventilation shaft that transmits the sound of falling raindrops from far above to deep inside the ship. So, it's raining outside. It's warm down here. I roll over and fall asleep again.

Monday, March 11th. We are woken up at 7 a.m. as we shall soon land in Harwich. I get dressed, pack up, and go upstairs. Everywhere people are crowding the corridors, and soon it will be impossible to get through. I push myself forward as far as I can towards the exit but get stuck in the dense crowd and wait like everyone else for the doors to be opened. Before I get stuck, however, I can reach a window for a first glimpse of the English coast, and recognize meadows bordered by hedges, a few isolated houses, and trees.

It's eight o'clock, the sky is clear, and it looks like it's going to be a beautiful day. Now we are informed which doors to use on which deck, and everything else we need to know to go ashore. It still takes quite a long time before the disembarkation finally commences and all the passengers are pushing and shoving as if there is a prize to be won for disembarking first.

I get to the clearance hall with the passport and customs control. There are three rows, one for travellers with British passports, one for EU citizens, and one for all other nationalities. I line up with the EU citizens and am quickly cleared through customs. The officer only takes a quick look at my identity card, gives a friendly nod, and then I've entered the country.

As is the case in the Hook of Holland, the trains in Harwich stop almost next to the ship. I thus do not have to walk far, and simply go down a flight of stairs. A railway employee checks my ticket, and I proceed to the platform from which the British Rail train is ready to leave. The compartment is not overcrowded, and there is no comparison with the crowd on the ferry. After a brief wait, we start moving and leave the port area. It is nine o'clock and I will be on the train for five hours before reaching Nottingham around 2 p.m.

One last look at the harbour. Parts of the huge ferry overlook the building. The train travels at a leisurely pace along the coast. I see fishing boats stranded by the low tide. We soon leave the coast and roll inland. The first stop is in Ipswich. Then it goes on past Ely Cathedral towards Nottingham in the East Midlands. The sun is shining and the sky is blue - it's going to be a beautiful day. We travel through a landscape that reminds me of Northern Germany. The Southeast of England is flat, canals run through the country, and wide fields accompany us.

After two hours, the landscape becomes hilly, and sheep graze on green meadows surrounded by hedges. In front of my window, a typical English landscape glides past, like out of a geography book. The peaceful impression of the rolling hills is intensified by the clear blue sky.

I'm happy to be here and have a positive feeling that I made the right decision. In Nottingham, the uncle of an English friend wants to pick me up from the train station and drive me to my host family in Derby. I don't know what the man looks like. However, he has a photo of me. Somehow we shall meet.

We are approaching Nottingham and I curiously look out of the window. This is going to be our new home for the next few years. The train pulls into the station. I'm nervous, now it's getting serious. Hopefully, I'll meet the man who's supposed to pick me up. Now the adventure really starts! In such a situation it is best to remain calm. When I remember my university exams, I know that I've already mastered many critical situations. In comparison, this is easy - I try to calm myself.

I get off the train at Nottingham railway station. For a city with approximately three hundred thousand inhabitants, it is quite small although this aspect is not that interesting at the moment. I'm looking around for a man who might also be looking out for me. The other travellers who left the train have long since passed me and disappeared up the stairs into the station building. I stand alone on the platform with my luggage, like a parcel that was ordered and not picked up. The train slowly starts to move again and passes me.

After the roar of the diesel engines has died down, there is a great silence. Where is the man who wanted to pick me up? He should show up. But nobody appears. There's no point in standing around on the platform, I better think of something now. Maybe he's waiting inside the station building. I pick up my luggage, turn around, make sure that no one is looking out for me, and walk to the stairs. As I climb them, I see a person strategically positioned at the top who appears to be waiting for someone. Maybe for me? The man must know me because he has a photo of me. Is it him? Yes, it is! He already recognised me. It certainly wasn't very difficult, because the two of us are the only people who are still near the platform at the moment. He greets me and asks how the journey was. I thank him for picking me up.

We walk to the car park and before we get into the car, he looks at me in surprise and asks if I intend to drive. "Me, why? Does it look like that?" The man is right, it really looks like I want to drive. If you want to get into a car on the driver's side, you probably intend to drive. This is my first encounter with left-hand traffic. Of course, I don't want to drive, "for God's sake, no!" I quickly switch to the other side and get in on the left.

We drive to the man's house in a suburb of Nottingham that almost exclusively comprises single-family houses with gardens. I still have to get used to left-hand traffic. Luckily I'm only a passenger. Especially when turning, I always have the impression of being on the wrong side of the road, and when another vehicle approaches, I fear the worst. In the house, I'm offered my first "cup of tea". While we drink tea, we talk.

After a good hour, it is time to leave for Derby to meet my host family. While driving, I survey the area carefully. In the south, I can see several power plants, otherwise, the landscape is very green.

We enter Derby, bypass the city centre and arrive at Darley Abbey. The tension is rising, soon we shall reach our destination. What will the members of my host family look like? What will the house look like? How will I be received? Questions, to which I will certainly receive an answer in a few minutes. We turn into a side street and drive through a pleasant residential area with large houses and beautiful gardens. After a while, we turn left into a driveway and the car stops in front of a pleasant house. If my host family is just as wonderful as everything here, then I can be extremely satisfied.

We get out and walk through the garden. Our arrival has

already been noticed, the door is open, I am expected. A woman with a very friendly appearance greets me. She also knows me from a photo. The man from Nottingham doesn't stay long but gives me his phone number, says goodbye, and leaves. The woman, her name is Irene, shows me my room. It is spacious and has a wonderful view over the large back garden.

Silence. It is quiet for the first time in many hours. Irene works downstairs in the kitchen, and I am alone in the room up here, standing at the window and looking out. My view sweeps across the garden down into a wide valley and up again to the houses of a residential area on the other side. Everything here looks different than at home. The houses, their windows, the church towers, and even the trees and meadows look different than I'm used to. It smells different – hard to describe – but it smells different here. I'm in a different country and many things are just different here. I'm sure I will discover these differences in more detail over the next few weeks. For now, I have to let all these new impressions sink in and slowly get used to them. I have a positive attitude towards anything new, and that's extremely important for this project.

After I'm done putting things away, thinking, and looking out the window, I head downstairs to the kitchen. Irene offers me a cup of tea and asks if I would like to go into town with her. This would be a good opportunity to get to know the way to the city centre so that I can find my way by myself tomorrow. I accept. Fifteen minutes later we are already on our way. Had I hoped we would take the car or at least the bus, I would have been disappointed. I would have liked a ride on the top floor of a double-decker bus, but we're walking. Why not? The weather is fine and the path through Darley Abbey Park also has its charms.

When crossing the streets, I am again confronted with left-hand traffic. I consistently look in the wrong direction before stepping onto the road. Instead of looking to the right, I automatically look to the left first. Every beginning is difficult.

First, we visit the city library as Irene has some books to return. On this occasion, I could have a user card issued to me. Surely I'd like to borrow some books during the next few years and, to do so I would need a user card, so I put my personal details on record. With a brand new user card from the city library, we continue walking through the city. I have to be careful when crossing the streets. Left-hand traffic! I still consistently get it wrong. Luckily nothing happens. However, Irene often holds me back, otherwise I would have stopped many cars today or landed under their wheels.

"Job Centre": black letters on an orange background. I will be visiting this centre more often during the next few days. We turn a few corners from the city library and arrive in front of the job centre. Irene just wants to show me the building so that I know where to go during the next few days. But, since we're already here, have time, and the centre isn't closed yet, why not go there today? I make a quick decision. Why postpone something that can be done today? During the following years, I (successfully) stuck to this basic idea.

We go up a flight of stairs and enter an open-plan office where consultants sit at several desks. After a while, it's my turn. A consultant takes down my details and asks about my education, professional career, and what kind of job I would like to have in the UK. I am asked whether I have a work permit. "Since Britain is a member of the European Union, I do not need a work permit", I reply. I encounter this question often during the next few weeks, months, or even years. The consultant looks at me, thinks about it, and then realizes that Great Britain is indeed a member of the EU and I would therefore not require a work permit. I'm surprised. Did she really not know that before, or had she never thought about it? This point has thus been clarified, I do not require a special work permit. If I have found a job, I can work in the UK. The current problem is just finding a job, and that's why I am here at the job centre. After my details are taken, I am told to come back tomorrow at 11 a.m. to talk to another consultant in more detail about jobs. I receive a card with the time and the name of the consultant. That's it for today.

Irene does some shopping, and then we return home. The weather is gorgeous. When we got home, I felt very tired. The walking, the conversation in a foreign language, everything takes its toll. I retire to my room, lie down, and try to process the many impressions that are pouring over me at the moment.

Half an hour later, I am called for dinner. After the surprises of the left-hand traffic, I should now also be introduced to the secrets of English cuisine. Hopefully, that's not too much at once. However, I am pleasantly surprised as Irene is a very good cook. Tonight we have roast beef, roast potatoes, crunchy vegetables and fresh salad. It looks very appetising and tastes delicious. The bad reputation that English cuisine enjoys on the Continent does not apply here at all. The food on the table is healthy, delicious, and tasty. I'm starving.

Although I was supposed to meet Irene's husband John at dinner, he had to attend a meeting tonight and thus I won't meet him until tomorrow at breakfast.

The day was exhausting and I'm very tired. Before I go to bed, however, I would like to give my wife a quick call to tell her that I've arrived safely. I ask Irene about a telephone booth nearby because I don't want to make a long-distance call from her phone. There is a telephone booth not far down the street. It's already dark outside. I walk down the street and look for one of those red, typically British telephone booths. Although I don't have to walk far, unfortunately, no long-distance calls can be made from there. I thus have no choice but to return and ask Irene to use her phone. Naturally, she lets me use it. Now the connection works. Marie and I talk briefly, and the morale is high on both sides of the English Channel. This was finally the last act for today. I wish my host family a good night and retire to my room.

Less than ten minutes later, I'm already in bed. Despite the tiredness, I find it difficult to fall asleep as there is too much going through my head. The new impressions have to be processed. The foreign language, the feeling of being far away from home, the new people, and the unknown that lies ahead of me. I lie awake, with faint light coming through the window from outside.

I look back on my life so far, including what I've achieved over the past few years and the decision to move to the UK. It has been four years since I left my hometown to study in the Saarland, a small Federal State in the west of Germany, where I lived together with Marie for more than three years. After completing my studies in business sciences and marketing, we married in the summer of 1983 and moved to Osnabrück in early 1984. I worked there as a sales representative for one year and attended an English language course in the evening. The lecturer, an Englishman, came to Germany fourteen years ago to live and work here for a few years to improve his German language skills. He started on ordinary jobs, worked for a transport company, rose professionally, and became a teacher at a language school. Today, he owns his own Language Institute and translates for local companies. Couldn't I do the same the other way around? I asked myself this question but kept the idea of going abroad to myself. One evening in November 1984, I asked Marie what she thought of the idea of moving to Britain for a few years. I expected scepticism. After all, we had something to lose. Marie worked as a secretary at the university, I had a good income as a sales representative and was able to use a company car. However, she looked at me and simply said, "Why not?" From that moment on, I knew that she was also interested in such an adventure and now nothing held me back. I planned, organised, and realized this project. In January 1985, I resigned. Now there was no turning back. Yesterday, I set out and now I'm here in the UK with a host family. Now it is time to put theory into practice. First of all, I have to find a job, and then a flat but this doesn't worry me at the moment. I feel strong, rely on my own abilities, and am convinced that I will find something.

Tuesday, March 12th. Since I fell asleep late, I rested a little longer this morning and arrived rather late for breakfast. I thus won't get to know John, Irene's husband, until tonight.

After breakfast, I walk into town to attend the 11 a.m. appointment at the job centre. It is a sunny morning and I'm full of energy; nothing can go wrong on such a glorious day.

I found the job centre without any problems and, thanks to the appointment I made yesterday, I don't have to wait long. The consultant is not particularly friendly, but professional. As a foreigner, I compete with many local unemployed and perhaps it does not make sense to her to help me, a German, to find a job when many of her compatriots are also looking for work. While I don't blame her, I am determined to find a job, no matter how dirty and hard it is. I shall stay here!

My personal data are recorded, and then a form has to be filled in. After everything is duly noted, she informs me that I'm now registered as a jobseeker in Derby and Nottingham for the next three months. In case of a suitable job offer, I will be notified in writing. That's all I can achieve for now. If I thought I could get a job today, that was pretty naïve. Nevertheless, my positive attitude does not suffer. I'll find something, I'm still firmly convinced of that.

It is just before noon and I leave the job centre and explore the city of Derby. In the shopping centre, I have lunch in a self-service restaurant, buy a local newspaper, and slowly make my way back. In Darley Abbey Park, I take a break near the Derwent River, enjoy the sunshine, the landscape, the whole atmosphere, read the newspaper, and skim the job vacancies. Who is wanted? Sales staff, bartenders, cleaners, temporary workers.

At home, Irene offers me a cup of tea and then we go through the adverts together. Irene says there isn't really anything interesting today. I notice the term "Employment Agency" and ask about it. These agencies are looking for staff. Perhaps it wouldn't be a bad idea to visit them during the next few days to find out personally what staff and qualifications they are currently looking for. I could start tomorrow. I take the addresses from the phone book.

Now I'm very hungry because apart from breakfast plus some fast food, I don't have much in my stomach. At supper, I meet John, Irene's husband.

Today was a busy day, and I'm very tired. My host family does not blame me for wanting to go to bed early, especially since I have a lot planned for tomorrow, namely to visit some employment agencies that seem very promising to me as they work on a success-oriented basis and will probably try harder than the job centre to find me a job. I shall know more tomorrow. Tonight, I have no trouble falling asleep.

Wednesday, March 13th. I'm up early and very keen to try my luck with the agencies. I walk into town and don't have to search very long to find the first one. "Service on a plate" is their slogan. I climb the stairs to the first floor, open a door, enter, and stand in a small office - nobody is there. I clear my throat once, twice.

A man appears. "What can I do for you?" he asks. How about a job offer? But it doesn't happen that quickly here either. He skims my CV, and I give him copies of my references. He delves into it and claims he understands some German. He's not particularly friendly. The office doesn't look very tidy either and, apart from him, no one else seems to be present. After some thought, he says he will keep the documents. If anything suitable came in, he'd let me know. I told him my current address and telephone number but cannot achieve anything further here. Unfortunately, that wasn't a good start, but there are more of these job agencies. Just don't get discouraged. The next one is definitely better.

I ask my way to the second address, and a passerby shows me where to go. Despite the heavy local accent, I understand him. That motivates me, and even the smallest feeling of success is important right now. The second agency is located in an office building and its premises are modern, leaving me pleasantly surprised. The young woman at the reception is very friendly. I should wait a moment, someone will come. It doesn't take long before I am fetched. First of all, I have to fill in a form. Patience is required, I'm told. I would be notified as soon as anything came up. Above all, I should study the agency's job advertisements in the local newspaper "Evening Telegraph" every day and call immediately if I'm interested in a job posting. Details of these vacancies would only be shared with individuals registered with the agency and registration is free. Nothing more can be achieved here either. To be honest, I was hoping for more from my visit to these agencies. However, there are still two more addresses left for today. Who knows, maybe I'll have better luck there.

By now it is lunchtime and I'm hungry. Like yesterday, I go to the local shopping centre and eat at the same fast food restaurant. Around 1 p.m., I start looking for the third agency.

Suddenly, there is a first kind of panic attack. It may not be as easy to realize our foreign project as planned. The famous question pops up: "What if?" What happens if I can't find a job? What happens if I can't find a flat? For a minute or two I feel afraid that everything might fail. The job search has not been very successful so far, and the prospects of finding a job are anything but rosy. Moreover, yesterday I learned from Irene that rented accommodation is generally hard to find, as the British prefer to buy houses rather than rent them. However, buying a house is impossible for me at the moment as I don't have that much money. These bleak perspectives fuel the sudden feeling of fear that hit me completely unexpectedly in the middle of the city. I try to calm down, knowing there's no turning back. The job in Germany has been terminated, as has the lease on our flat in Osnabrück. I have no choice but to move on. Of course, I could return to Germany, but this would mean that I have failed. I find it difficult to think positively but succeed nonetheless. I definitely have to maintain my confidence, and my belief in success, as otherwise I will fail. I try to calm myself: today is only my second day in the UK.

I find the third employment agency. The manager is friendly and invites me to his office. I inform him about the current situation and enquire about job opportunities. My education, especially my qualifications, seems to impress him. "It should be possible to find something", he then says. He promises to enquire about vacancies at some companies. The man makes a professional impression. He certainly doesn't just say this to get rid of me quickly, but perhaps also sees a good opportunity for himself to earn money through a successful placement. He will notify me. I hand over the copies of my certificates and CV to him. Although I wasn't able to get a job with this agency either, the conversation gave me an enormous boost. At least this man has recognised that I have something to offer and even thought I should be able to find a job.

The hint of weakness, the crisis from earlier, is over. I didn't give up. On the contrary, the offensive has only just begun.

It is early afternoon, I cannot find the fourth agency, and feel far too tired to keep looking. I should go home and study the job advertisements in today's afternoon paper. After a cup of tea, I take my time to look through the job advertisements. I'm glad not to be alone. Irene advises me which job offers seem serious and which ones I should stay away from. After skimming through the offers, we find that today there is very little that is interesting. However, some offers could be worth following up on. For example, there is an advertisement for a chocolate factory that will soon open a new plant in the surrounding area and will probably need workers. Since I am willing to accept any kind of work, I should contact them. Since I still have some problems following the strong local accent, I ask Irene to call and she does me the favour. After she finished talking to them, she notified me that they would send me a form that I should fill in and send it back. At least that's a modest success.

We discover another interesting job offer. A company is looking for a sales representative and one can find out more by calling them. Again, Irene does me the favour of calling and the result is a job interview for tomorrow at 9 a.m.

The day ends better than it began. I visited three employment agencies, handed in my documents, got over a motivational crisis, will be sent a personnel form during the next few days, and have an interview tomorrow morning. If that's not a partial success after only two days in the country!

However, the biggest highlight of the day comes in the late afternoon. I'm in my room, sitting at the table, arranging addresses and names of agencies and companies, when Irene calls me. I go downstairs. She just found out from a friend that there is a flat for rent. Would I be interested? We could go right now to see it. Of course, I'm interested! The day just keeps getting better.

Less than fifteen minutes later, we are on our way in Irene's little blue Mini-Cooper. A few minutes' drive north of Darley Abbey is the small village of Duffield and once there, we turn onto a side road. Pretty cottages made of natural stone are lined up to the left and right of the relatively narrow lane. Irene turns into a side lane, and then we're already there. The residential area is quiet and my first impression is very positive. The house in which the rental flat is located is relatively old. From the lane, it looks rather basic, although, on the garden side, large windows convey British flair. There are four flats in the house and the rental property that is currently available is on the first floor.

Irene meets her friend and we look at the flat together. The eye-catcher of the spacious living room is a formerly open fireplace in which a gas stove is now integrated. From the multi-part bay window, you have a fantastic view of the garden and there is a mighty chestnut tree right in front of the window. I immediately fall in love with this room. Fully furnished, it will be really cosy here. The kitchen is opposite the living room and its condition is sobering. A worn floor, an aged gas stove that is partially singed, and an unappealing sink. The window glass facing the lane has a crack and is poorly glued. The first impression of the kitchen is not exactly positive. But, with a little paint and cleaning products, a lot can certainly be changed here. The corridor leads to the bedroom. This room is in extremely poor condition! The wallpaper is peeling off. According to the landlady, there were problems with the roof, and water had penetrated the outer wall. In some places, there is a gap between the wall and the bottom lath. The roof, I am assured, has now been renovated, but the walls still need to be repaired. There is no heating or gas stove in this room. The bathroom is small, dark, and decorated with worn wallpaper that is peeling off at the edge of the bathtub although a bit of colour will improve a lot here, too. The rental price for this flat with two rooms, kitchen and bathroom is £88 per month, due to the residential area. I have concerns about the kitchen, the bathroom, and especially the bedroom with the damaged walls. On the other hand, I really like the cosy living room with the marvellous view. It's love at first sight! The neighbourhood is also positive. The place is rural, but the city of Derby with its approximately two hundred and fifty thousand inhabitants is only about ten kilometres away and thus one doesn't live completely "behind the moon" here. The rental price is reasonable for the location.

Now the crucial question: Will I get the flat at all, or are there other interested parties? There are! But since the landlady is Irene's friend, I have a kind of reference advantage which I should use. My disadvantage at the moment is that I don't have a job yet and don't know when and, above all, where I'll find one. Should I find employment in Derby, the flat would be fine. However, if I find work in Nottingham, it would be a long way from here. I'm in a quandary. I like the flat and know that I can't be choosy with the limited availability of rental accommodation, but should also be sensible because I have to find a job first since it is only when I know where I earn my money that I can look for a flat close to where I work. If I were to commit to this flat now, afraid someone else might snatch it from me, and then find a job a long way from Duffield, I'd be in real trouble. So, what shall I do? I try to be diplomatic as in no way do I want to lose the flat through thoughtless comments. I thus mention the problem of finding a job and the fact that it is not yet clear where exactly I shall be working. I know Irene is on my side. She will certainly support me if her friend doubts whether I can afford the flat. The reference advantage works. The landlady understands my current situation and seems to like me. She's interested in tenants who won't cause trouble and she'll keep the flat free for me for a week. During this time, I can try to find a job. If I find one and am still interested in the flat, I can rent it. That's a fair compromise and I couldn't have achieved anything better. Now it's time to find a job as quickly as possible, and if that works out, then I shall have a flat on top of it. That would be a huge success. But it is not achieved yet. I still have to find an opportunity to earn money during the next few days which won't be easy, as the last two days have shown.

Back in Darley Abbey, I meet a man from the neighbourhood. He works at Rolls-Royce, which is currently the largest employer in Derby alongside British Rail. Maybe he has connections or knows if and where someone is wanted. In any case, he could enquire. He is very helpful and promises to ask around. I give him a set of copies of my certificates plus my CV and ask him to hand them over to the Human Resources (HR) department and he promises to do so tomorrow. It is an opportunity and I have to try everything. Moreover, it is also about the flat whose living room fascinated me so much. I would love to move in there.

What a day! I suddenly realize how very tired I am and almost fall asleep in front of the TV. I can only keep my eyes open with difficulty. It is time to go to bed because tomorrow I have another eventful day ahead of me, not to mention the job interview. The fear is gone, and confidence has returned. There's no way I'm going to give up.

Thursday, March 14th. I mustn't oversleep this morning because I have to be in town by 9 a.m. to attend the job interview. A bus takes me to the city centre. John gave me a street map, and the orientation works. I turn the last corner onto the street I'm looking for and am met with a desolate sight! The houses are run down, and some have bricked-up or boarded-up windows.

There is dirt all over the pavement and street. How on earth is a reasonably reputable company supposed to be located here? If I had expected a lot from this interview, disappointment is now slowly rising. A few streets before it still looked very promising. There were houses in which one might assume offices. But to be honest, this sight is devastating! I would love to turn around and run away but then I pull myself together. Now that I'm here, I will find out what kind of company and job it is.

I walk on, look for the house number, and find it on a building that is in just as bad a state as pretty much everything on this street. I go inside and stand in semidarkness. A few people are sitting at a table in a corner opposite the reception. I am registered, and the organisation seems to be working. After about five minutes, an employee asks me to follow him. We walk along a narrow corridor and enter an office at the end. What a difference to the rest! This room is quite presentable. Carpeted floor, pictures on the wall, large desk, leather armchairs. The man who invited me to the interview stands up behind the desk, shakes my hand and asks me to take a seat in one of the leather armchairs. He introduces himself as the general manager, is quite fat and seems to love golden jewellery which glitters pretty much everywhere on him. This makes me suspicious. This man is certainly looking for someone who is supposed to talk customers into some product. And that's exactly how it is. A car wash is to be sold at the front door. We talk for half an hour. The man is professional and polite. Since I've only been in the country for a few days and don't yet speak the language fluently enough to be able to convince customers, this job is not ideal. We both agree. But the conversation was definitely an achievement. They are looking for someone for a specific job and I was invited for an interview.

It is almost noon, and I take a break. In the afternoon, I visit the job centre. There are cards with job offers on blackboards. I take my time and study as many of these offers as possible. Maybe there is something for me too. However, I'm not the only one who is interested as many people are looking for jobs. You can clearly see that in this room. I compete with practically all job seekers without special qualifications, which means finding very simple jobs. I can't even get to some of the blackboards as they are densely surrounded and thus approach the panels that are not crowded. I like the system. The individual cards briefly describe the job and specify the required work experience and the hourly wages which allows one to get information without having to talk to a clerk. The offers are subdivided according to work areas. There are jobs in sales, in the office, in manufacturing or in the care sector. Even though I would be interested in some of them I do not have the experience that is required and thus I don't even ask but continue to look for work that doesn't require any special experience, with the help of which I could gain a foothold in the UK during the coming weeks and months.

A warehouse worker is wanted, in addition to a mobile park ranger, and another warehouse worker. I take the three cards from the blackboard, approach one of the clerks and briefly describe my situation. The young woman is very friendly. We discuss the offers. Unfortunately, the first job offer of a warehouse worker has already been taken, while the second position requires special experience that I unfortunately do not have. The third offer, the mobile park ranger, is still available. No special experience is required. If I want to, the clerk explains, she can give me the job poster's address. It certainly couldn't hurt to stop by there once. I receive the address and off I go.

Again, the street map is very helpful. I find the location, hand in the card from the job centre, and receive a form to fill in. This takes some time because I have not yet filled in many forms in English and some expressions are unfamiliar to me. I ask my way through, have some words explained to me, and am finally done. When I return the form, I am told that many people are interested in this job, and I will be notified about my application in a few weeks. This doesn't sound very promising and I don't have high hopes. Firstly, this is a public vacancy in the City of Derby which would certainly be given to an unemployed local, and secondly, in a few weeks, the flat in Duffield will surely be let to someone else. I need a job right now, and not in a few weeks. The application is running, I'll let it run, but will definitely continue to search intensively. There's no time to lose.

I returned to the city centre and wanted to take the bus, but eventually decided to walk. The excursion through the park to Darley Abbey is pleasant, walking calms me down, the sun is shining, and I need some distraction. There is still no breakthrough, my job search is still unsuccessful. The mood drops. Doubts begin to arise again as to whether it was the right decision to come here. The more I think about it, the more doubts I have, and the more restless I become. Now it's time to stay motivated, fear must not win. Tomorrow is another day with new opportunities that I will seize.

At home, I drink a cup of tea together with Irene and John and eat some biscuits, which is reassuring. I don't see things quite so negatively anymore and explain what I did today. They notice the disappointment in my voice, try to encourage me, and think I'll find something if I keep looking as hard as I have been so far. The conversation motivates me, and my optimism slowly returns.

However, that evening, my positive attitude was once again put to the test. The neighbour with whom I left my documents yesterday and who wanted to ask Rolls-Royce if there were any vacancies stopped by for a moment. Unfortunately, he doesn't have good news. No employees with my qualifications are currently being sought. He forwarded my documents to certain people but doesn't think anything could be found. Some employees at Rolls-Royce were only recently laid off. I am disappointed because I had high hopes regarding this opportunity and it is gone now. I'm finding it increasingly difficult to believe in success.

Then, Irene has an idea. Not far from here, just down the street, across the Derwent River, is the Darley Abbey Mill and various repair shops, craft workshops, and other small businesses have recently settled there. Maybe it would be a good idea if I stopped by there tomorrow and directly asked about jobs. I like the suggestion. It comes at the right moment and puts me back on track. Instead of just introducing myself to job agencies, I should approach some companies directly. The thought of trying out this strategy tomorrow is very motivating.

After dinner, we sit in the living room. It is already dark outside. Suddenly, I feel the need to be alone. During my academic studies, I often took long walks to study exam material, or just to think and this always helped me to make the right decisions. Hence, I feel the need to get some fresh air now to reconsider my current situation. I hope my host family will understand and doesn't feel offended. No problem. I don't need the door key, because it won't take long.

As I walk along the lane outside, I take a deep breath, which relaxes me. I've been in the UK for four days now, and have been searching intensively for a job during the last few days, but haven't been able to find anything suitable yet. Although the job search is turning out to be more complicated than expected, I still do not think about giving up. These are simply new facts that I did not know and therefore could not plan for. I have to adjust to these new facts and come to terms with them. So far, I've only visited job agencies and, except for the one interview, I have not yet approached any company directly. This needs to change. Perhaps a new strategy will bring the much-needed breakthrough. Despite the difficult situation regarding rental properties, I already have one prospective flat. The result of these four days is not too bad. I must not allow myself to be discouraged by setbacks, and must not lose hope that my plans will be successful. There is only one way for me, namely the way forward. Going back is not possible. I relax, am determined not to give up, return to the house, have a brief chat with my host family, and go to bed.

Friday, March 15th. I am up early this morning and am keen to start looking for a job. The procedure planned for today is completely new to me. I have never gone from door to door to look for a job. How will people react? Will I be able to find work?

After breakfast, I set off full of hope and self-confidence. It is only a few minutes' walk to Darley Abbey Mill. In front of me, on the other side of the Derwent River, lies an impressive industrial area from the time of the Industrial Revolution. Some of the red brick buildings are four stories high. In the background, a few chimneys rise into the sky but are no longer in operation. In the past, the Derwent River provided the electricity for the factories, but textiles are no longer made here today and small handicraft businesses and repair shops have settled on the site. I want to visit all of them today. Maybe there is a job for me.

I cross the river on a small bridge and enter the industrial area. The barrier at the entrance has been raised and no security guard is to be seen. In the first building, there is a small machine tool manufacturer, and behind it, a repair shop. Now it's getting serious! So far, everything has only been theoretical planning. Now it is time to put theory into practice. I will knock on every door and try my luck. Asking doesn't cost anything and I am sure no one will throw me out. I have nothing to lose. Even the most perfect planning is of no use if you don't have sufficient courage to implement what you have in mind. I shall muster that courage now.

I decided to start my job search in a small machine tool factory, walk to the first available door, enter, encounter noise, running machines, and a few workers, and ask one of them about the HR department. He shows me the way, is busy, and doesn't really care much about me. Nobody in this workshop seems to notice the stranger who shows up and walks through the building.

I find the HR office, gather all my courage, open the door and enter. My knees are slightly weak, and I try not to appear as nervous as I actually am right now. The office is small, with two women sitting at a desk. I addressed one of them: "I'm from Germany, would like to work in the UK for a few years, and am looking for a job. Are there any vacancies here?" The two women react slightly surprised. Such a request is certainly not presented to them every day. However, they are friendly and helpful and want to know more about me, where exactly I come from, and why I want to work here. The situation becomes more relaxed, and I become calmer, appear self-confident. Unfortunately, there are currently no vacancies at this company, and although the two women would be happy to help me there is nothing they can do for me at the moment. However, they gave me a form that I should fill in and return. They assured me that if anything came up in the near future I'd be notified, but I don't have high hopes. There is nothing here and there will be nothing in the short term.

Although I did not find a job in this instance, I gained some valuable life experience. For the first time, I directly visited a company abroad to look for a job. The first steps have been taken, now it's time to continue. There are other companies here, so which one should I visit next?

I keep walking, get to the next machine tool company, go to the first door, and enter. There are machines in the workshop, it is loud, stuffy and smells of oil. I ask the first employee I meet about HR. He tells me that there is no personnel office but I should ask "the man over there" as he might know more. I follow his advice and speak to the man in question who seems to be a supervisor or even the boss. When I ask about possible jobs, his answer is "No!" There are no vacancies. There's nothing to be done, and I'm out again. This was the second attempt, and like the first, it was unsuccessful.

There is a small colour factory right next door. New attempt. I already have some routine, at least my knees are not as weak as on the first attempt. I enter a narrow stairwell, reach the first floor, and find myself in a large workshop in which several people, mostly women, are working. There is a lot of activity here and it smells of glue. The employees stand or sit at tables on which they cut or glue something. At first glance, I can't tell what it is exactly. Radio music can be heard all over the place. I ask the person closest to me about the HR office. There is no such office, but I should ask the head of the department, his office is just around the corner. The woman shows me the way there.

The door is open, but I knock anyway. The man is talking to someone. I wait a few minutes, and then he offers me a chair in front of his desk and asks what he can do for me. How about a job, for example? Could he offer me one? I briefly describe my current situation and hand him a copy of my CV. He reads it carefully. It is not common here that someone – especially a foreigner – suddenly shows up and asks for work. He is surprised but friendly and wants to know more about me. Our conversation lasted about fifteen minutes and he informed me about the company, its products, and what kind of jobs there are. As for work, I assure him that I'm ready to take on any job, whatever it may be. This seems to impress him. He thinks for a moment, then calls the supervisor and asks her to perform a test with me. I follow the woman back into the workshop. There I am shown the products that are manufactured here. Small pieces of wallpaper are glued to pre-printed forms, which can then be found as sample sheets in department stores.

The test I am about to take consists of two parts. The first part is a colour test to figure out if I might be colour-blind, and I have no difficulties with it. Then, I have to glue some wallpaper patterns neatly one below the other on a form. This also works without any problems. The supervisor seems to be satisfied with my work, looks at the samples, then at me, and says that I could have a job although it wouldn't be a permanent job, just temporary work. If I was interested, I should contact her on Monday at 9 a.m., and she would then assign me to a job.

I can hardly believe it. Am I dreaming or is it reality? I've just been offered my first job in the UK. Great! My first job abroad and I found it all by myself. I'm incredibly proud of that. Taking the initiative brought a breakthrough, and it took me less than two hours.

I want to share this positive news immediately, but no one is at home. Irene must have gone into town. I remember the flat. Only two days have passed since the viewing and it was to be reserved for me for a week. I have to call the landlady to inform her about the job and that I want to rent the flat but I do not know her phone number nor when Irene will return.

I have to do something as I am full of energy and don't want to waste a minute. How do I get from Darley Abbey to Duffield? By bus. So, on to the next bus stop. I don't have to walk far. When do the buses leave? No timetable is available. I have to wait. Luckily it doesn't take long until a bus appears. Two days ago, I drove the route with Irene in the car, so I know roughly where to get off and which lane to walk to. If I can't find the house, I can always ask my way around.

The bus ride takes around ten minutes. I get off at the stop on the main street of Duffield and find what I am looking for after just a few minutes. The landlady lives with her family in a new house, in the middle of a wide garden, a little below the old house with the flat. I walk down there and ring the bell, anxious to inform her about the news. Nobody opens and I am disappointed but there is nothing to be done.

However, now that I am here, I should use the time to get a first impression of the area, because apart from the flat itself I did not see much during my first visit. I walk towards the end of the village. Attractive houses line the street, surrounded by lovingly tended gardens. Now in March the trees and bushes are still bare. How wonderful it must look here in summer. I like the neighbourhood right away. It is beautiful and I still cannot believe that I might soon be able to live in this wonderful environment. However, as long as it is not entirely certain whether I will be able to rent the flat, I try not to get excited too soon as this would only make the disappointment worse if it does not work out. If the landlady would only come home, then I would already know today.

I return to her house, but unfortunately, there is still no one there. I take another tour, another half hour goes by, and still no one is at home. If I am unlucky, this can go on for a long time and I thus decide to abandon the attempt and return to Darley Abbey. After all, I was promised that the flat would be kept free for me for a week and I have to trust that the landlady will keep her word - I have no choice.

Back in Darley Abbey, nobody is at home either and I don't seem to be able to share the joy of my first job with anyone, although I am so proud of it. I sit in the living room and turn on the TV. Half an hour later, Irene returns. I intended to wait for a little while before telling her about the day's events, at least until she finished unpacking but did not succeed. As soon as she was in the house, I literally blurted out the news. However, despite all the euphoria, I must not forget the flat. If possible, I would like to conclude the rental agreement today and ask Irene to call the landlady to let her know that I have found a job and would like to rent the flat in Duffield from April 1st. She does me the favour of calling and so I already know this evening that the flat will become our new home. The rental contract will be sent to me next week, and I can move in in two weeks.

I lie awake late that night, too much is going through my head. Two days ago I was afraid the project might fail, and today the situation has changed completely. I found my first job and can rent a flat in a pleasant neighbourhood. It was worth not giving up when the first difficulties arose. The breakthrough had to come after everything I had done in the past few days. The "Project UK" appears to be secured for the moment. I've been in the country for five days now. At the end of this first week, I have a job and a flat. On the whole, it was fairly quick. Sure, I was lucky, maybe very lucky, but I also took many risks. If you don't take any risks, you can't win anything either. However, there is still a lot to do, and although this is only a modest beginning, I am confident. Whatever is to come, I will face it. That is what I am thinking tonight. What the future will bring, good luck or bad luck, is still unknown, but I am not afraid.

The weekend arrives and I deserve a break. Since I was fully focused on finding a job during my first week, I have not seen much of Derbyshire yet. This first weekend should now be entirely devoted to discovering my new adopted home. Matlock, around twenty miles north of Derby, is said to be very pretty.

On Saturday morning, I take one of the red Trent buses. We pass Duffield, Belper, Wirksworth, Cromford, and Matlock Bath. The landscape is so typical of England, rolling hills, meadows bordered by hedges, and isolated groups of trees. The villages with their typical houses and church towers also immediately show which country you are in. Imposing cliffs tower on either side of the valley near Matlock Bath. I let all the new impressions sink in and imagine how beautiful this countryside must be in summer.

We reach Matlock. There is a supermarket just opposite the bus station. Today I have time, there are no appointments to keep. I roam the market with interest. I always enjoy discovering new things in supermarkets in foreign countries, unfamiliar goods, product names, packaging, and prices. I have done this many times in France, and today is my first chance to do so in the UK. Now that it is lunchtime and I am feeling hungry, I buy a "German Sausage", some bread, milk, and two apples. With this "food package" in hand, I start my discovery tour.

The ruined Riber Castle towers high above Matlock and one should have a wide panorama of the surrounding landscape from up there. I walk uphill for a good hour. While the sun shines at first, dark clouds gather later – it is amazing how quickly the weather changes – and ultimately it starts to rain. Shortly after, thick hailstones hit the ground before it started to snow. However, the snowstorm does not last long either and the sun is shining again by the time I reach the top of the hill. During this hour-long ascent, Great Britain shows me what its weather has to offer. So far, I have not encountered any fog, which is what the country is supposed to be so famous for. On reaching the top of the hill, I found that I was right about the outlook. From up here, the walker has a wonderful view down to Matlock and over the Pennines mountains. Next to the "Riber Castle" there is a small zoo with lynxes, birds, and farm animals, as well as a model railway and a museum with old cars and motorcycles. Suddenly, it starts to snow again and thick flakes accompany my descent into the valley. However, the renewed snow flurry quickly subsides and changes from sunshine to rain.

Back in Matlock, I revisit the supermarket to stock up on a personal supply of groceries that I want to keep in the cupboard at home. A few groceries of your own give you at least a slight feeling of independence if, like me, you don't have your own flat at the moment. As helpful as my host family is, I need at least some sense of independence, even if at the moment it just means being able to eat something without having to ask for it. A bus takes me back to Derby in the late afternoon.

On Sunday, I attend the service at Derby Cathedral. At the end of the service, the parish priest shakes hands with everyone at the exit. I was already noticed as a new face and he asked me where I was from. We talk for a while, he knows Osnabrück, has friends there, and wishes me all the best for my project.

Today is Mother's Day in the UK and bouquets of flowers are sold in front of the cathedral. I buy one. Irene's son Peter is currently far away in Germany, as is my mother, and I thus give the bouquet to Irene on behalf of Peter. Irene, in turn, is to a certain extent representing my mother today. She is very happy about it.

At lunchtime, there is the traditional Sunday meal consisting of roast beef, roast potatoes and Yorkshire pudding. It is my first Sunday lunch in the UK and tastes fabulous.

In the afternoon, Irene and John invited me for a walk. They want to show me some of the surrounding area. We drive into the mountains of the "Pennines" and hike across a ridge. On one side, the terrain drops off quite steeply, while on the other, a plateau covered with heather extends as far as the eye can see. The views are terrific!

That evening, I lay awake again for a long time. Tomorrow is my first day at work. Now it's getting serious. How will the new colleagues welcome me? Will they accept me? Can I cope with the foreign language? How will the job be? Questions surge through my mind and will not let me rest even though I am very tired. I've got some stage fright now that it's all really starting.

FIRST JOB AS A CASUAL WORKER IN A COLOUR FACTORY

Monday, March 18th. I am supposed to report to the colour factory at nine o'clock this morning. I get up just before 8 a.m., have breakfast, and then set off on foot, walking for ten minutes. Shortly before 9 a.m., I arrive at the factory.

The large workshop is full of people, and my new colleagues all seem to be there already. I stand around, feeling a bit lost in the room, and no one approaches me. Then I saw the supervisor who did the test with me on Friday. She also recognised me and came over and greeted me. She assures me she'll take care of me right away but first has to distribute today's work. I wait a few minutes. The supervisor returns, asks me to follow her, and leads me to a table where three women are already working. They stick wallpaper patterns on a sheet and I should watch them for a moment and then try to do it myself. The wallpaper samples are picked up with the right hand and pulled through a small machine powered by an electric motor before two rollers apply glue to the underside of the samples. Afterwards, the sample pieces are grasped again with the left hand and glued to the right place on the sheet. This process is carried out by the three women at insane speed, hundreds, maybe even thousands of times a day. Will I ever be able to do it that quickly? Right now, I can only watch with admiration.

After a while, it is time for me to try it myself. I also receive one of these little machines, fill it with glue, and start working. Every beginning is difficult. Either one of the samples gets stuck between the two rollers or falls into the glue tray because I cannot pick it up fast enough with my left hand. My colleagues are amused by my efforts, and this is how first contact is made as they show me how to do it. Step by step, I improve my bonding technique although there is often either almost no glue on the back of my samples or too much, causing my sample sheet to smudge. However, I work on the technique and I am confident that my new colleagues will gradually introduce me to the secrets of proper glueing.

It gets better after an hour. Although I am still a lot slower than the others, at least I have already completed several sample sheets. From time to time, the supervisor comes by to see how things are going. She seems pleased with my pasting skills so far, so I am too.

As far as conversation is concerned, little is happening at the moment. Music from the radio fills the room, and the three women at the table are talking to each other. So far, no one has included me in the conversation although this was good at first as I was focused on coordinating the various movements. However, now that I have managed to do this to some extent, I'd like to chat a bit. The reason that I am here is not to learn glueing techniques but to improve my language skills and thus I often take a look at the women working around me. When this doesn't bring the hoped-for success, I take more looks and in the end just look. I even almost forget to work. But, apart from a friendly smile, still nothing happens. For these people, I am simply a foreigner and they do not know what I am actually doing here. Maybe I should start a conversation myself to break the ice. If I wait until the others start talking to me, I can certainly wait a long time given the alleged reserve of the English. However, I have to be careful to not be too intrusive, especially at the beginning as it always takes a certain amount of time before a working group accepts you as a new colleague.

I cautiously start a conversation with the words: "It's not as easy as it looks. You've already finished a lot more sheets than I have." This first attempt to establish contact isn't exactly responded to with enthusiasm, but rather with reserved comments such as "It'll be fine" or "It's not bad at all for a start." Everything just takes time. My colleagues will certainly soon become curious and ask me where I come from and what I am up to. I just have to be patient and wait until they start a conversation.

At 11 a.m., a bell reminds us of the breakfast break which I am told will last fifteen minutes. All employees leave their workplace and flock to the door and I go along with them. We climb two floors up a flight of stairs to a lounge with several tables and chairs. Everyone sits down, sandwiches are unpacked, and water is put on for tea. I sit down at a table where young people are playing cards and watch them. They play with great enthusiasm. Although nobody talks to me, I have to be present, and must not isolate myself. At the end of the break, the bell calls us back to the workshop.

Lunch break is from 12.30 p.m. to 1 p.m. There is no canteen, but one can buy something to eat from a small shop just around the corner and I bought two sandwiches and a chocolate bar. We eat in the lounge. I sit down at the young card players' table again. Incidentally, I am now being asked for the first time where I come from. There you go, my colleagues are becoming curious. I mention Osnabrück. Some have heard of the city, as Osnabrück is Derby's German twin town. My colleagues started taking an interest in me and wanted to know why I came to the UK and where I live. They try to classify me but they are still unsure. How is it that a German comes to Great Britain and volunteers for a simple and poorly paid job just to learn a foreign language? This doesn't mean much to them because no one around here speaks any language other than English. They don't understand my personal goal. They probably think I'm a little crazy and keep playing cards.

After the lunch break, we return to the workshop. By now, I can handle the small machine, and my wallpaper patterns are beginning to become more and more linear, and no longer slightly offset as they were in the morning after my first attempts. In the afternoon, the supervisor transfers me to a larger work table and assigns me to a new job. Five women work at this table. I received a finished sample to see what the whole thing should look like and then I was given blank sheets, wallpaper samples, and a new little machine.

Piecework wages are paid here, which means we are ultimately paid based on the number of completed sheets. There is a target per hour and if I do not achieve it, I get paid less whereas if I finish more, my income will be higher. However, the specifications are so high that my bonding technique still needs to be improved a great deal during the next few days if I want to get rich here. At the end of each day, the number of sheets that each person has completed is noted and, today, I only managed a little more than half of the target per hour. As a result, I only earn half the hourly wage, which is already very low anyway. But, at least I earned something. It's a start and, for the time being, I am pleased to even have a job.

In the afternoon, some attempts at establishing communication also succeed and the colleague sitting across from me begins to ask questions. She wants to know my age, whether I'm married, or have children - everything that women generally want to know. I am slowly becoming integrated and a conversation ensues across the table. The others are now also starting to ask questions, and accepting me as a new colleague. The people of Derbyshire speak with a very strong local accent which I am still having to get used to. It is difficult for me to follow the conversation of the women at the table, especially since they speak very quickly. However, I am able to pick up some new words, ask questions, receive explanations, and am well on the way to improving my language skills.

Music blares from the radio throughout the day and you automatically start humming along and cannot get some of the melodies out of your mind. While the conversation between my colleagues mainly revolves around "who did what, with whom, and where", they also talk about football, horse racing, well-known singers and actors, cars and money. In any case, I get used to the local accent and learn about the everyday life of my colleagues, their interests, joys, and sorrows.

At 5 p.m., we finish work. Everyone cleans their little machine so that it can be used sparkling clean again the next day. The remaining glue is poured into a large container from which the machines are refilled the next day. After the workplace has been cleaned and the time card stamped, I can go home for the day.

That was my first working day in the UK. I did a reasonable job, was able to establish some first contacts, learned the work and the daily routine, and am beginning to settle in. From tomorrow on, I shall no longer be "the new bloke" who everyone carefully observes, but will already start to belong to the working group.

I return home, satisfied. This job may not be a dream job, but it is the first step in the right direction. I will improve and expand my English language skills through daily communication with my colleagues, and that is the main goal of this stay abroad. That evening, Irene and John were naturally very curious about how things went at work and there were many positive things to tell. After recounting the day's news, we sit in the living room and watch TV. However, I soon realized that the physical work had made me very tired and it didn't take long before my eyes started to close. I wish them a good night, go to my room, and soon fall asleep.

Second day at work. Shortly before 9 a.m., I'm back at work, preparing my little machine, filling it with glue, and picking up the sheets that are to be dealt with today plus the wallpaper samples. Then I start working, and hopefully, I will be a little bit faster than yesterday. The daily routine is just the same: bonding, breakfast break, bonding, lunch break, bonding, and closing time. Cards are played again during the breaks. A young girl is now working across from me. She is a big fan of a famous pop singer who she seems to be in love with. Her shrill voice is getting annoying. I got along much better with the other colleague who was working across from me yesterday.

During the following days, I improved my working speed but still did not reach the target and thus I am only earning approximately eighty per cent of the wages that the others are getting. When the others play cards during the breaks, I now play along from time to time. A colleague was absent due to illness and I asked if I could step in, which was approved.

Actually, I like it here quite well, if it weren't for the colleague with the shrill voice directly opposite me. For most of the day on Friday, she only talks about which bars she will go to on the weekend and what and how much she will drink. I think at her young age she should rather focus on her education than work in a colour factory and drink too much on weekends. What kind of future does such a young person have? Luckily, that's not my problem.

Friday is payday and I received the first money that I have earned abroad. However, the amount is not overwhelming, only £25 net for a whole week's work is in my pay packet, whereby this is better than nothing. If I reach the target during the next week by working faster, I shall certainly earn more. Although one cannot get rich with a job like this, I am glad that I have it.

I received the rental agreement this week. The flat in Duffield is mine now, and nobody can snatch it from me anymore. As a precaution, I have Irene check the contract before I sign it, to be sure that there isn't anything negative hidden somewhere. You never know. However, everything is fine. I sign it, send it back, and can move in there in two weeks.

Now that I am earning money, especially since I have to pay monthly rent plus additional costs, I need a current account. However, getting one is easier said than done, because the banks in town are already closed after my working hours and only Saturday morning remains. I know from Irene that one bank is open until noon on Saturday mornings and it doesn't really matter which bank I go to anyway. Apart from brisk marketing slogans, they are all the same in the end. However, as only this one bank is open on Saturday mornings, and I need a current account, I open one there.

I brought 2,000 D-Mark (Deutsche Mark) in traveller cheques with me which is the first seed capital that I invest in our stay abroad. At the current rate, I get approximately £500 for it, put £250 of that into my new current account, and the rest in equal halves into a savings account at the same bank and into a UK postal savings account. I am currently paying Irene £10 a week for meals. In the future, the flat will cost £22 rent a week plus £13 extra costs. I estimate £15 a week for groceries, although this is very tight, which would amount to £50 weekly spending. In contrast, my current income is between £25 and £30 per week and thus every week I have to plug a financial hole of £20 to £25 from my savings. However, this was already taken into account when planning the project.

In addition, there are still 3,000 D-Mark available in my German postal savings account, from which I can withdraw money at the main post office in Nottingham if necessary. The rest of my financial means remain in an account in Osnabrück. If the project fails, there would still be enough money in Germany to return. I don't want to invest more than 5,000 D-Mark.

At present, 400 D-Mark are required each month out of this investment capital. Together with my current earnings, I would have twelve months to improve my income so that I no longer have to inject any money and only then will the project pay for itself. I still have a long way to go. Will I succeed?

March 1985. I am doing fine at work, communicating with colleagues, improving my language skills, getting faster on the job, and increasing my weekly income to £35. The foreign language is constantly around me, and nobody speaks German. This is a great advantage, as I am forced to only speak English and every day I learn new words, terms, expressions, and idioms. My colleagues are very friendly and explain new words to me.

The job is ok, and only the colleague with the shrill voice at the work table is annoying. My hope that she will soon be reassigned to another workplace turns out to be in vain and thus, if she doesn't get assigned to another table, I will have to. This seems to be the only solution. I make a firm resolve to move to another table and, the next morning I show up very early, dismantle the little machine at my previous place and move it to a free spot at the other end of the room. My colleagues do not even notice, as many of them change tables to do other work, and thus I can do the same. My new neighbour is a very nice woman with whom I can have a reasonable conversation.

I call Marie once a week. She is relieved that I was able to find a job and a flat after such a short time. However, I don't tell her about the problems and concerns during the first week so as not to worry her unnecessarily. Everything looks fine at the moment. As planned, she will quit her job in Osnabrück on June 30th.

To a certain extent, our foreign project resembles a strategic operation. One goes ahead and forms a kind of bridgehead. Reinforcements are ready across the English Channel. If the project fails after a certain number of weeks, one can return.

At this stage, the bridgehead has been set up and the site provisionally expanded. Now I have to persevere until my wife follows. While withdrawal is still possible during this time, after we've both moved to the UK, there is no turning back, at least for the planned two years.

I learn of the existence of an "Osnabrück Club" in Derby where friends of the town twinning meet. I decided to go there one evening as I can perhaps make some contacts there. Who knows, maybe I'll meet influential people and thereby improve my job situation. However, my hope quickly turns out to be unfounded. I assumed people would be interested in me. After all, I moved from Osnabrück to Derby to live and work here for a while. But no one was really interested in me that evening, and I did not receive the hoped-for support in finding a job.

After a slide show about Osnabrück, small groups stand at the bar, drink beer and wine and chat. I stand around, a bit lost, and try to start a conversation with some of those present but, apart from some "small talk", not much happens.

I won't stay long, this is a waste of time. If I had expected a lot from this evening, I must bury this hope now. There is no point in relying on others and hoping that people of influence can help me. It is best to rely only on your own abilities. Anyway, that's exactly what I'm going to do now.

FIRST RENTED FLAT IN DUFFIELD, DERBYSHIRE

Saturday, March 30th. This afternoon, I am moving into my new home in Duffield. Although the tenancy doesn't officially start until April 1st, I can already move in today, whereby "moving in" is probably not the right expression at the moment because I don't own any furniture yet as the furniture will only arrive here in about three months when Marie leaves Osnabrück. Strictly speaking, I am thus only occupying the flat today. Since I do not yet have any furniture of my own, my host family kindly made some available to me temporarily: a table, a chair, a mattress, a sleeping bag, an electric heater and some crockery and cutlery. I don't need more at the moment.

John drives me to the flat and helps me carry the loaned items upstairs. One last handshake, then I am alone and, after just three weeks in a foreign country, I am independent again.

A great silence surrounds me. Nobody speaks, nothing moves. During the last few weeks in my host family's house, there was always someone there, I was never completely alone. Now all of a sudden it is completely different. If I don't speak, nobody speaks. If I don't move, nothing moves. Anyone who has suddenly been all alone knows this almost eerie silence. I have to do something, mustn't get sentimental now. Just about happy to finally be in my own flat again, I can't capitulate to the silence now.

I walk from one end of the flat to the other, making noise on purpose to drive out the silence, set up the table, find a suitable place and put it in the living room in front of the large bay window with a view of the garden. Then I sit down in the only chair I have, at the only table in this otherwise empty room, and look out into the garden. How beautiful it will be here in summer when everything is green and blooming. Once the furniture is there, we can arrange our new home comfortably. I can well imagine it all. However, until then, there are still a few months ahead of me, which will certainly not be easy.

I carry the mattress, the sleeping bag, and the electric heater into the small bedroom. This room, in particular, needs to be renovated in the coming days and weeks. Due to the moisture that has penetrated the walls, the wallpaper stands out from the rest of the masonry. A solution is required here. There is also work to be done in the bathroom and kitchen to make them more homely. But I'll have plenty of time over the next few months and can paint and fix up the entire flat. I certainly won't get bored.

After my few belongings are stored away in the flat, I walk through the village. It is starting to get dark, and I stroll around for a good half hour, exploring the immediate vicinity of my new home. Everything is completely unfamiliar which gives me the feeling of being in a small clearing in the middle of a huge, unknown forest. Everywhere is new territory. The area slowly becomes more familiar until you finally feel at home. I am really curious to discover the unknown - but not all in one day. The half-hour is enough for the moment. I now know a little bit about the surrounding area.

When I return to the house, it is already dark. Back in the flat, I realize that there is no electricity yet, and thus so there is no light. I sit in the dark with no candles and no flashlight either, and thus have no choice but to crawl into my sleeping bag. However, sleep is out of the question that evening. The first night in a new surroundings is always something special. I lie awake, dead tired, but cannot fall asleep. It is quiet in the house, too quiet. Then, I finally dozed off.

Suddenly, something woke me up. A TV was turned on in the flat directly below me. I try not to listen, but the device must be directly below me. Now a horse race is probably being commented on, the reporter's voice becomes faster and louder, and the horses seem to be approaching the finishing line. How are you supposed to sleep here? How long will the neighbour watch TV? Peace finally returns, the device is switched off, and I doze off again.

Sunday, March 31st. At around eight o'clock, my neighbour turns on the TV again. I get up and have breakfast. Irene gave me some bread and a jar of jam. Tomorrow evening after work I have to stock up on some groceries.

I sit at the table in the living room, eating a few slices of bread with jam and drinking a glass of water. The sun is shining outside, and the window is open. My first breakfast in the new flat.

This Sunday is relatively quiet. I read a book in the morning and go for a long walk in the afternoon. A narrow country road leads me out into nature. There are a few magnificent houses here, and their residents must be extremely wealthy. How lucky I am to live in this area. After about ten minutes, I pass the last house. The road is now bordered on both sides by hedges so typical of this country. I am moving on a ridge. To my left, a valley widens with green meadows bordered by hedges, isolated groups of trees and, here and there, a farm. Far over there, on the other side, the land rises gently again, only to fall into another valley, which cannot be seen from up here. To my right, the view is different. The land slopes down more steeply, and in the valley, there is only space for a farm with a few meadows and pastures. Behind it rises a ridge, the first foothills of the "Pennines", the mountain range that stretches from here up to the Scottish border.

I reach Hazelwood, and a few houses accompany the street. The weather is changing, dark clouds are gathering in the northwest. It might rain soon and I don't have an umbrella with me. That shouldn't happen in England! I start heading back home.

Although I actually wanted to introduce myself to the neighbours today, I am tired after the long walk and have decided to postpone this action until tomorrow. In addition, one should not be too intrusive during the first days after arriving and I definitely do not want to give the impression of being pushy.

Tonight, I eat my remaining groceries. I must go shopping tomorrow. After that, I read. I brought a lot of books with me, as German-language literature will probably be difficult to find here.

It is getting dark. Unfortunately, I cannot turn on the light because there is still no electricity and I thus go to sleep with the last daylight. I am curious how this second night will go. Do I have to listen to a horse race or something similar again? The TV is on, but the noise level is tolerable. Around 11 p.m., it is finally quiet.

I sleep a lot better during the second night. Today is Monday, and a new working day is starting. A bus takes me from Duffield to Darley Abbey. From the bus stop, it is only a few minutes walk to the Mill.

9 a.m., work starts. The small machines start moving and all my colleagues start glueing their samples. After the breakfast break, the head of the department appears and shows me a business letter from a German company, which unfortunately is not written in English but in German. He therefore doesn't understand the text and asks me for a translation. As I owe him this first job, I promise to do so.

In the evening I return to Duffield by bus. There is still no electricity in the flat, although the landlady has promised me that she will take care of it.

Tonight, I intend to introduce myself to the neighbours in the house.

First, I knock on the door of the flat opposite. A young woman is supposed to live here, but nobody opens the door. No chance today.

I go downstairs and try the ground floor where the flat with the TV set directly below my bedroom is situated. I knock on the door. Footsteps can be heard, and an elderly man opens the door. I introduce myself to him as the new tenant. He nods politely and invites me in. We drink a cup of tea and talk. I tell him where I'm from and what I'm up to, and he listens with interest. In between, I look around and discover the TV set. It is almost exactly below the spot where my mattress is one floor up and thus it is no wonder that it's annoying when it's switched on. However, I don't mention anything. The man is friendly, I'm new and don't want to start our neighbourly relationship with a complaint. I'll just have to get used to it unless I find another place to sleep. I mention the electricity problem. Without being asked, the man kindly offers me a whole box of candles to use until there's light.

I return to my flat. Thanks to the candles and some matches, I will not sit in the dark tonight. I will visit the flat next door tomorrow, it will not run away.

Tonight I want to translate the business letter. To do so, I put a few candles on the mantelpiece, some by the window, and two on the table in front of me. The atmosphere is very romantic. The large room is slightly illuminated by the flickering flames, while the dark garden rests in front of the bay window. You could almost think you were in a castle. The candles are reminiscent of a time when there was no electricity at all. Suddenly, I'm no longer annoyed at not having an electric light. I am sitting here by candlelight in an old house in the middle of England. A poet might have sat at a table by the light of flickering candles a long time ago. Unlike him, however, I am not writing any romantic poems or exciting novels tonight, but rather translating a business letter into English. It is an offer of new materials for wallpaper, fabrics and yarns. The content is very technical and I often have to look up special terms in the dictionary. My first translation job in the UK was by candlelight in my new living room. Some candles have already burned out quite a bit and are beginning to flicker violently. I replace them with new ones. At least I have a whole box of candles, which is sufficient for several evenings.

It is pitch-dark outside, almost eerily quiet. Nothing moves except the flames of the candles, which flicker one way and then the other. I sit in the semi-darkness and do nothing, just let the silence affect me. I am calm and content. I made the right decision. It was good to have come here. Whatever difficulties still await me in the future, tonight, at this moment, I am determined to find a solution to everything.

I am tired, time to slip into my sleeping bag to be ready for another increase in my adhesive performance tomorrow. For once, the TV isn't on tonight and I fall asleep quickly.

My earnings increase during the next weeks as I complete more sample sheets. However, the current costs are still far from being covered. My colleagues have accepted me, I belong to the work-group and can expand and improve my vocabulary. Some of my colleagues also show interest in learning some German words, unfortunately mostly curses and other swear words, but still.

On a Saturday morning, I visit a building centre where I buy a bucket of white paint, some tools, and whatever else is needed to renovate a flat which costs me half a week's wages. In the afternoon, I start with the renovation.

To begin with, I take care of the small room I am currently

sleeping in and the mattress is moved to the living room, where there is enough space. The wallpaper and plaster that are protruding due to the water damage must be repaired. This turns out to be rather difficult, but it can be done with a little manual skill.

The following weekend, I started painting the room as the cement had dried and the damaged areas were fixed.

During this week, I also introduce myself to the neighbours of the second flat on the ground floor. An elderly couple lives there. They are also friendly and immediately offer me a cup of tea and a piece of homemade cake. Both are still very energetic for their age. Her name is Rose, and his name is Leslie. We start talking, and they find my project extremely interesting. Leslie offers to call my wife from his phone. I politely decline because I don't know if he realizes how much such an international call costs. However, I make a note of his phone number. If Marie needs to call urgently, she can reach me there.

I also meet the young woman in the flat next door. She seems to be quite shy, only opens the door a crack, and a long conversation does not develop. I'm sure she's a bit wary, which is understandable for a single woman.

Now that I know all the neighbours, this flat is slowly becoming my new home. I'll be painting all the rooms during the next few weeks. Every day when I get home from work, I pick up the brush and work for an hour or two. On the weekends, I renovate during the afternoons. In between, I drive to the building centre a few more times to get more paint. After the bedroom, I paint the bathroom, kitchen, and hallway - all white. By the time I am done, the rooms are almost unrecognisable: they are now clean and fresh. The company I work for gave me a large leftover piece of wallpaper, large enough to replace the old fish pattern wallpaper in the bathroom. I installed a new mirror and the bathroom looks brand new. In a few weeks, Marie will come to visit for several days and everything has to be set up by then. I am right on schedule with the renovation work. Hopefully, she will like the flat as much as I do.

Friday, April 12th. First setback! All casual workers, including myself, will be laid off at the end of next week due to the current poor order situation. Should the situation improve, the company will consider hiring staff again in a few weeks. This not only affects me, but also some of my colleagues, mostly young people without special qualifications. However, this doesn't bother them as they will simply apply for unemployment benefits. In contrast, the situation is not that easy for me. Firstly, as a foreigner who has only been in the country for a few weeks, I would not receive any unemployment benefits, and secondly, I didn't come to the UK to be unemployed.

The changed situation is also a new challenge that brings new opportunities. The monotonous work and the low salary are really not very interesting. Somehow, now is the time to find a better job. The temporary dismissal has created a situation that compels me to react. Although I might be able to return in a few weeks, in the meantime, I should try to find something better. I see the new situation positively. After all, I've been in Britain for six weeks now, know my way around better, and have already been able to make some progress with the language. I really want to look for a new job.

During the weekend, I continue to renovate the flat, think about a strategy for the second direct job search, and draft a letter of application that I intend to mail to various companies whose addresses I took from the local newspaper. I am still working at the colour factory until the end of next week. During this time, I will apply for new jobs in writing. If this approach is unsuccessful, I will set out again myself and visit companies directly.

On Sunday afternoon, the weather is ideal for going for a walk and exploring the area further. I leave Duffield and walk along the main road towards Belper. As I enter Milford, just a mile from Duffield, I discover a company on the left-hand side of the road. I could try my luck here next week. On the way to Belper, I noticed other small to medium-sized companies where it would also be worth applying for a job. The closer I get to Belper, the more companies there are. I count a total of thirteen. Although it wasn't my intention to look for new potential employers this afternoon – I just wanted to go for a walk – this is a helpful coincidence. On the way back, I am already busy planning my second job search. With such a large number of companies, the chance of finding new employment should be fairly high. Full of confidence, I can barely wait to go out and try my luck.

The last days in the colour factory passed quickly - I worked here for five weeks. As I leave Darley Abbey Mill for the last time, I am not sad, as I know that something new is on the horizon. I can decide for myself how to proceed and this motivates me. I feel free and strong. Somehow, I'm glad things turned out the way they did as I probably would not have dared to so quickly trade the relative security of a salary, however small, for the adventure of another uncertain job search. The temporary release thus practically made the decision for me.

During the week, I have already sent off several written applications, but have not yet received any replies. However, I won't just wait for the postman, I will take action myself. Friday is my first day without work and I will use it to visit the thirteen companies in the Belper area.

Friday, April 19th. This morning I get up early, have a little breakfast, pack copies of my CV and certificates into my shoulder bag, and set off. The weather is on my side, and a bright blue sky and warm sunshine accompany me. Nothing can go wrong on such a glorious day, success is literally in the air.

I walk from Duffield towards Milford, feeling free, and able to determine my destiny. I sense no boundaries, do not depend on anyone, and only rely on my strength.

On the outskirts of Milford, I reach the first company. Despite my initial feeling of confidence, every beginning is difficult, and I'm a bit nervous. As with the first job search, this nervousness has to be overcome. Success boosts self-confidence. The office building is surrounded by a small park. I enter and stand at the reception, nobody is around. There is a phone on the table. I pick up the receiver and dial the number provided. A woman's voice answers. "I would like to speak to someone from HR," I reply. I am told I should wait. At least I'm not going to be turned away immediately. My confidence rises. After a few minutes, a woman appears. She is friendly and asks me to follow her to a conference room where I hand her a copy of my CV and put the folder with my certificates on the table. She seems impressed but also amazed that I show up here and ask for work. She introduced herself to me as the secretary of the managing director, who is currently travelling on business in the USA. That is why she cannot tell me anything specific at the moment. However, she would like to keep my documents to show them to her boss as soon as he gets back. After that, she says goodbye, wishes me all the best and promises to inform her boss. When I'm outside again, I don't have a new job yet, but it was a partial success. I wasn't turned away, the secretary kept my certificates, and she was impressed. I have to use this positive mood to continue with my job hunting.

Right across the street is a Garden Centre. During the summer months, I was told, casual workers were sometimes hired there. It may not be summer yet, but it would definitely be worth asking.

The nervousness has subsided. Most people are friendly and helpful even if there are no jobs. So far, I have only encountered appreciative, encouraging words everywhere. I cross the street and enter the centre. The man behind the counter is pretty taciturn. I ask for a job, he shakes his head. There are currently no vacancies. There is nothing he can do for me. After this brief encounter, I am back on the road again.

There is another factory complex in Milford. The entrance gate is open, I walk through it, cross the courtyard and head for the office building. A security guard watches me. I ask him about HR. "Wrong place," he says. The HR department is located at the Belper plant. I should try going there. "No problem, I intend to go to Belper anyway." My morale is still very good. I've visited three companies, had one partial success and ten chances remain. The probability of finding a job is still relatively high.

The next company is already waiting at the end of the village. Here, however, I cannot even access the company premises, as the security guard won't let me pass. However, I can call the HR department from the gatehouse. Such phone calls usually lead to nothing – one is sent away relatively quickly – and it is no different here. I briefly speak to an employee who immediately lets me know that there are no job vacancies.

I continue walking along the main street and although I sense a slight feeling of disappointment, there is no point in quitting. There are still nine opportunities left. Three other companies have settled near Belper. I try my luck with the first one. Here, I can enter the office building without any problems, which is an advantage. I present my request to the secretary at the reception, who asks me to wait for a moment. I sit down on a chair under a large plant. After a few minutes, an employee from the personnel office appears. He is in a hurry and one can clearly feel it. I briefly explain why I am here and he replies, just as briefly, that there are currently no vacancies. At least he doesn't talk for a long time but gives a clear answer. There is nothing to gain here either.

However, another potential employer is waiting right next door. Here, too, there is no security guard to stop me and I reach the reception through the main entrance. There is a telephone on the table. I dial zero, and a voice answers. I tell them that I am looking for work, but the answer is negative. There are no jobs here either.

I hang up, leave the room, cross the street, and approach the third possibility. There is a security guard here who won't let me through. I can call HR, but that doesn't help. There are no jobs here either and again, I have to concede defeat.

I draw an interim balance: seven companies have been visited, and the result so far has been rather disappointing. However, there are still six opportunities left, and I will pursue them.

I continue walking along the road into Belper. The confidence of this morning begins to wane, and resignation sets in.

I reach the next company. It is small, practically consisting of only one shop floor. However, it is in a new building. Why walk by just because the company is small? I have nothing to lose and should make use of every opportunity. I enter, and there is no one in the office. I step outside, walk around the shop floor, find another entrance, hear voices, meet two men, talk to them and ask for a job. But, there are no vacancies here either.

Luckily, at least the weather is on my side. The sun is warm and flowers are blooming everywhere. How terrible a rainy, cold, grey November day would be. But, it is spring and I can still motivate myself. There are five companies left and, who knows, maybe success is not far off.

I approach the centre of Belper and see another large company on the right side of the street. The security guard lets me pass. It is almost unbelievable, but he actually lets me through and even tells me how to reach the personnel office. However, this attempt also ends at reception. Unfortunately, the information from the receptionist regarding jobs doesn't sound very promising, but at least she calls HR and asks someone to be sent to see me. My hope of finding a job here diminishes, progressively declines with each passing minute spent waiting, and reaches zero when a young woman finally shows up just to tell me there are no vacancies. I can feel myself despairing inside. Why are there no jobs? Although I would be willing to accept any kind of work, there was nothing, absolutely nothing, to be found. Wherever I go, I always receive the same answer: "No jobs!" This is frustrating!

I pull myself together - there are still four opportunities left - cross the street, approach an administration building that has certainly seen better days, enter the reception hall through a revolving door, and immediately feel transported to another era. Two elderly women are sitting at the reception desk, and the telephone exchange can be seen in the background. Both women are friendly and extremely helpful. I briefly describe my request. They show interest and find it very captivating that a young German seems to have lost his way in this small town. However, I am by no means lost. I am here quite consciously and hope to be able to stay, that is, if I finally manage to find a job. The two consider who I could approach. Unfortunately, the person who would be most suitable is currently not there. Then, one of the two ladies picks up the phone, dials a number, hands me the receiver and explains that I should present my request to the person who will be in touch right away. Although I don't believe in the success of telephone calls, I pick up the phone and try my luck. A woman's voice answers and I tell her that I am looking for a job. At the other end of the line, there is a brief thoughtful silence. Unfortunately, at the moment she cannot tell me anything definitive, because the man who could help me is out of the office. This man really seems to be very important, because the two women at the reception had already referred to him. "When is he coming back?" "He should be back in the office in about an hour." I thank her and put the phone down. Well, he'll be back in an hour, the man everyone here thinks is the right person to talk to. Therefore, I should show up here again this afternoon. Through the revolving door, I step out into the sun again.

There is a chocolate factory just around the corner where I applied for a job a few weeks ago. Now that I am here, I should take the opportunity to ask what happened to my application. The personnel office is located in an office container next to the street. I enter and have no luck. I was told that my documents had been filed and that if there were any vacancies, I would be notified. This doesn't sound very promising.

Further down the street, I come across the branch of a German company. The woman responsible for HR would be happy to help, but can't offer me anything suitable at the moment. At least this request was worth a try.

Only one of the original thirteen companies remains. I am on my way to take advantage of this last opportunity. Although I am despondent, I intend to finish what I have planned for today. I wanted to visit thirteen companies, and at the end of the day, it should have been thirteen companies. The last chance is located at the other end of town at "Belper East Mill", an imposing factory building made of red bricks, which today stand out particularly intensively against a deep blue sky. The gate is open, and I walk in and approach reception. This is where today's last attempt to find work ends. The receptionist lets me call HR, but that doesn't get me anywhere either. The usual answer is: "Sorry, no jobs". That's it for today. Nothing particular came out of thirteen chances.

I am hungry. After all, it's already past noon and I hardly ate anything this morning. My positive attitude tends towards zero. I am too tired to analyse the situation now, and thus return to the town centre, enter a supermarket and buy something to eat. Two sandwiches for now, and a few tins of soup, packaged fish, some sausages, bread and biscuits for the next few days. Outside the shop, I sit down on a bench in the sun. I am starving! After the sandwiches, half the pack of biscuits also disappears into my stomach. Then, I feel better. But, I had enough for today. After all the failures, I don't need another defeat and I don't really fancy a second visit to the company where I didn't meet the right person earlier today and am supposed to come back after the lunch break. Thoughts circle my mind. On the one hand, I am frustrated, on the other hand, I have nothing to lose. Why miss an opportunity? I pull myself together and decide to go back.

I set off on my way, carrying the shoulder bag full of groceries. Through the revolving door, I re-enter the semi-darkness, and the two ladies at reception recognise me immediately. "The person you should talk to is here now," they tell me with a smile. "He just came back a few minutes ago." I don't have to wait long either, and an elderly gentleman appears and asks me to follow him to his office.

I sit down on a chair right in front of his desk. The person who is supposedly the right contact for me is friendly and asks where I come from, what education I have, what I've done for a living, why I came to Great Britain, and what my plans are. I proceed to answer all of his questions and briefly describe my current situation. He listens with interest and wants to know if I have a work permit for the UK. "As an EU citizen, I don't need such a document," I reply. "Oh yes, of course, that's right. Great Britain is indeed a member of the European Union," he remembers. As was the case at the job centre, the knowledge of Britain's membership in the EU does not seem to be particularly well-developed with my interlocutor. However, now it occurs to him again and that is at least positive.

Does he have a job for me or not? That's pretty much all I am interested in at the moment. He now informs me about the company, the products, the export countries and the group of companies. And? Jobs? Are there any? Or am I getting nothing here too?

Suddenly my shoulder bag with the groceries, which was on the floor in front of me, tips to the side and a tin of soup starts to roll towards the desk. I stop it with my foot just in time and slip the cheeky object back into my bag as inconspicuously as possible. I am embarrassed about the incident, but fortunately, it doesn't seem to have been noticed.

My counterpart now mentions that the Federal Republic of Germany is an important export country for British textile companies. That is interesting! Does that mean that German language skills are needed here? I've been sitting in this man's office for quite some time, he takes his time and gives me detailed information about the company. This looks good. The hope of maybe getting a job is increasing by the minute. There must be something to be found here, otherwise he would have put me off long ago and sent me away.

Unfortunately, he can't offer me a qualified job, he remarks. But casual workers are sometimes needed in the warehouse. He wants to check whether I could be employed there, hands me an application form, and asks me to fill it in and send it back immediately. Did I really just score here? He hands me his business card. To my surprise, one of the directors of this company is sitting in front of me. It is all too good to be true. I hope I didn't fall asleep on the bench in front of the supermarket and am just dreaming about it all. But it is actually reality, I am not dreaming, everything is real.

On the way back to Duffield, I could jump for joy and hug anyone who came my way. What a great feeling it is to achieve some success! Even though I don't have the job yet, things look promising. The director himself took some time for me, he was interested in my CV and asked me to fill in the application form as soon as possible. I'm already dreaming about what kind of work would await me and what opportunities for advancement might result from it. The defeats of the morning are suddenly forgotten. My motivation barometer has shot up enormously.

When I get home, I sit down at the table, the only one I have, and fill in the application form. Not a minute should be wasted. I add a couple of copies of my certificates and carry the envelope to the post office straight away.

What a day! It began with the realistic belief that there were good chances of finding a job at thirteen companies. Then, one disappointment followed another. After thirteen direct enquiries, I still didn't have a job, almost wanted to give up, but luckily didn't. Then came the breakthrough. Now in the evening, I have high hopes that I've found my second job in the UK today. However, I will probably have to wait a while until I get a positive answer. In any case, I want to use the time and will continue to look for work.

This weekend, I am going hiking with Irene and John in the nearby mountains. I also inform them about my recent job search and they keep their fingers crossed for me.

Monday, April 22nd. I continue to visit companies, this time in Duffield.

At first, I stop by a small colour factory where I get through to the HR manager straight away. He is friendly, knows Osnabrück, and has already visited friends there. I try to use the positive mood for myself, to turn it into a job, so to speak, but in vain. The man would like to help me, but unfortunately, there are currently no vacancies.

I keep searching. Next, I proceeded to visit the head office of the local building society which is situated in an old manor house plus some new adjoining buildings. I reach the reception through the main entrance. Everything here is modern and sparkling clean. "I would like to speak to a member of the HR department." To my surprise, the receptionist asks me to wait, she will notify the HR office. After a few minutes, the HR manager himself appears. I presented my request, and the conversation lasted about ten minutes. He tells me that he cannot offer me a job right away and gives me an application form to fill in. Even if there is currently no suitable position, he still wants to keep my documents.

Next, I visit the local laundry, but without success. The garage right next door doesn't need anyone either. On the way back to the flat, I poke my nose into the office of a small timber company. They can't offer me a job here either.

That's it for today. Five attempts, and no job found. The result is sobering, morale is falling, and frustration is rising. But, I am not giving up! There are certainly new opportunities tomorrow. I have to be patient. However, I cannot just sit around doing nothing and have to keep searching, as time is passing quickly. In a few weeks, my wife will be coming to the UK for her first visit. By then I would like to have a new job, otherwise, the situation wouldn't look particularly favourable and that might worry her.

Tuesday, April 23rd. Today, I intend to visit Rolls-Royce, probably the most famous address in Derby. Aircraft engines are manufactured here. It would be a dream to get a job at this world-famous company. I haven't applied to Rolls-Royce in writing yet, because I wanted to keep this dream alive.

A bus takes me to the south of Derby. In front of the factory premises, I look for the main entrance, and head for a multi-storey administration building but don't get far. Two security guards stop me and ask who I would like to meet. "An employee of the HR department," I explain truthfully. "The personnel office is not in this building," I am told. I should go back down the street, HR is located in the big long building on the left side. I follow their directions, find what I am looking for, encounter other security guards, and have to register. I am asked whether I have an appointment. That's it then because I don't have an appointment. "I'm from Osnabrück, Derby's twin town in Germany, and I'm looking for a job", I explain, trying to save the situation. It actually works. One security guard is impressed and begins to talk about his last vacation in Germany. His positive memories benefit me now. I slowly begin to gather new hope. He picks up the phone and calls HR. Could I possibly get an appointment? This hope is abruptly dashed. The HR manager responsible for employees is currently on vacation. Bad luck! Such damn bad luck! Everything started going so well. I almost got past that security guard. And today, of all days, the person who is so important to me is on vacation. I can hardly believe that this attempt has come to such an abrupt end. I am terribly disappointed.

However, the friendly security guard has a small consolation. "There is another HR manager for commercial employees who is not on vacation", he says. However, his office is in a different part of the plant, about half a mile from here. So, I set off again. The office is located in a building that can be entered from outside the factory premises, which is already positive. I climb the stairs to the first floor and enter a larger room, but nobody is there. Voices can be heard through an open door. I clear my throat a few times to draw attention, but no one appears. After a more breathy "Hello!" a secretary appears and asks what I want. "I would like to speak to the HR manager, is he present?" "No, unfortunately, he isn't. Why do you want to speak to him?" she continues. The woman is not particularly friendly. "I'm looking for a job." "There are currently no jobs at Rolls-Royce", she replies. I should come back in a few months, maybe there will be some then.

That's probably the end of my dream of being able to get a job at this world-famous company and I have to accept it. One HR manager is on vacation, the other is not available at the moment, and there are currently no job vacancies at all. However, I am determined to try again sometime in the future.

That's it for today. I am fairly frustrated as it is difficult to accept this defeat after the hopeful euphoria. A bus takes me back to Duffield. When I get home, I realize how tired I am, eat something, and go straight to bed. Tomorrow is a new day, and I shall keep trying.

Wednesday, April 24th. I am waiting for the postman, hoping for a positive answer from Belper. Unfortunately, in vain.

I am taking a day off from the job search to think about the current situation, to build up new motivation, and, above all, to avoid more defeats. I write some applications to companies whose addresses I took from the local newspaper. My hope of finding a job through written applications is not very high, but you never know. In any case, I do something.

Then, I continue to renovate the flat and go shopping. Marie will be visiting for the first time on Wednesday, May 1st, and will stay until Saturday, May 5th. That's already in a week. I want her to like the flat. Hopefully, I will have found a new job by then. Being completely without work would certainly not be an ideal welcome gift. I still have a week left and will continue to search intensively tomorrow.

Thanks to the break, I am motivated again, and yesterday's frustration was soon forgotten.

Thursday, April 25th. After breakfast, a bus takes me to Derby again. Today, I want to look for jobs in the city centre.

First, I intend to check job opportunities at British Rail, the second-largest employer in Derby. The porter at the British Rail administration building calls the HR department, and an employee picks me up and takes me to a conference room. However, after a brief conversation, the result is negative. A job at British Rail is currently not possible.

I tried British Telecom but found out that its HR office is located in Nottingham.

I visit the job centre to study the current job advertisements. One of the jobs on offer could be suitable for me, a warehouse worker is wanted. I take the card with the job description, enquire, and receive an application form that I'm supposed to fill in and send to the company concerned. Naturally, I am competing with a lot of unemployed locals for this job and, as a foreigner, my chances are certainly low.

In the afternoon, I buy the Evening Telegraph and look through the job advertisements. A furniture company is looking for employees for the showroom. According to the address provided, this company is located in the city centre of Derby, which is very close to where I am at the moment. I'll set off immediately and find the company. Once there, I enquired about the job and was told that it was already taken.

Afterwards, I dropped by the employment agency, where I had a conversation with the manager during my first week in the UK. He remembers me and gets the file with my documents. Unfortunately, to this day, he hasn't been able to find anything suitable.

Why do I still rely on others? Either I find a job myself or the foreign adventure will fail.

I return to Duffield. Another day has passed, and I've been searching for a job, but haven't succeeded. Tomorrow, I will continue - I'm still a long way from giving up.

I've been sleeping on my mattress in the large living room for quite a while now. It is much quieter here, and no TV disturbs me when I fall asleep. In the evenings, I hear the voices of my neighbours Leslie and Rose in the flat downstairs when they talk. This is not disturbing, but pleasant. It makes me feel like I'm not completely alone. I am seriously considering turning the large room into a kind of common "living/bedroom". There is enough space to place our double bed with the two bedside tables in one part and use the rest of the space as a living room. No TV would disturb our night's sleep and the small room could be used as a dining room.

Friday, April 26th. Again, I am waiting impatiently for the postman. Today, there must finally be an answer from Belper, whether positive or negative. The interview took place a week ago and my documents were sent immediately. It cannot take that long. The postman arrives around nine o'clock, but there is still no answer today. Something must have gone wrong. Everything had looked so promising. I was able to speak to one of the directors, he took his time and seemed interested. I immediately sent the application form along with other documents. Why isn't there an answer? I decided that I wouldn't wait any longer but will investigate the matter myself today. Now, I want to know, even at the risk of losing this opportunity by taking the initiative. I set off immediately.

The bus takes just under ten minutes from Duffield to Belper. I am nervous! In a few minutes, the only real hope of work I have right now could be gone. I would be very disappointed, but have to be prepared. However, I simply must know.

I pass through the revolving door at the main entrance and enter the reception area. The two ladies remember me. The director is there, and they will notify him that I would like to speak to him. I take a seat and wait. The tension rises. I need a job and here I am so close. Hopefully, nothing goes wrong now. I don't have to wait long, my conversation partner appears, greets me warmly and invites me to his office. He had received the documents and wanted to reply today. He keeps talking and it is like music to my ears. He was able to find me a job. At that moment, I feel a huge sense of relief. These are the moments in life that you never forget, that you remember forever and ever. This is the breakthrough! Success is finally here after all the intense searching. I have been looking for a job for a week now, except for one day off. I had to put up with numerous defeats and was often disappointed and frustrated. However, I did not give up. There was always a new day and a new morning that allowed me to overcome the disappointment of the previous day and embark on a new courageous attempt. The courage and perseverance to ask again and again was ultimately successful.

What kind of employment is it? The job is relatively simple. Temporary workers are wanted in the warehouse once in a while to help out with storing and retrieving the numerous products. The company in Belper is part of a large textile group. The salary is slightly better than at the colour factory, but you cannot get rich from it either. I will earn £45 per week. After the deductions, that leaves around £35 net. However, this amount does not depend on a target specification but represents a regular fixed amount which naturally is more pleasant than the previous piecework wage. Since the new income is insufficient to cover all expenses, I still need money out of my savings. However, it is at least a slight improvement, and therefore a step in the right direction. I can start on Monday at nine o'clock.

In bright sunshine, I walk back to Duffield and enjoy the sweet feeling of success. I was able to find a new job just in time for my wife's visit, although it was really tight. Today is Friday, and she's arriving in five days.

Now it is time to prepare everything so that Marie likes it here just as much as I do. I mend something here, paint a bit there, sweep, wipe, clean. Everything has to look nice and inviting.

In the afternoon, I take the bus to Allestree, a suburb of Derby, and shop at a supermarket. To celebrate the day, I treat myself to a delicious piece of cake, sit down on a bench and, for the first time in days, feel something like inner peace. The stress of the job hunt subsides. I am no longer one of the numerous job seekers but have a job again.

For a while, I sit and watch the passers-by. It is nice to just sit there, have time, and know that one is on the right track.

In the evening, I share my joy with Irene and John. They will provide a second mattress, a second sleeping bag, and a second chair for Marie so that everything is prepared for her visit.

Despite a few disadvantages, our new home is extremely comfortable and it has a very special flair. I love sitting in the large room with the window open, looking out over the wonderful garden. It is beautiful here, peaceful and quiet.

During the last days before Marie's arrival, I cleaned the flat thoroughly and bought some flowers, which immediately gave the room a positive aura.

SECOND JOB
AS A WAREHOUSE WORKER
IN A TEXTILE COMPANY

Monday, April 29th. My first working day at Belper. I was greeted personally by the director who offered me the job. He accompanies me to the new workplace. We walk through the main building, cross a well-lit courtyard and arrive at a large warehouse where men and women work at packing tables. I count eleven people. On the left side of this hall are long, high shelves on which products are stored. To the right are several packing tables, each with four people working. The director leads me to one of these tables and introduces me to an elderly man. His name is Bill and he will instruct me in my new job.

Each worker receives several orders in the morning that he has to pick. To do this, you have to be familiar with the warehouse and know where which item is stored according to type, colour, and size. This is not as easy as it sounds, because many items are also stored in adjoining buildings. For me, as a complete beginner, it seems almost impossible at the moment to be able to find my way around this maze of aisles and shelves. But, every beginning is difficult and I am enthusiastic about the job and glad that I found it in the first place.

During the first few days, I mostly worked with – and talked to – Bill. He is very helpful and shows me around. Slowly, my other colleagues also started to take an interest in me, whereby this happened much quicker than it did at my first job. This is certainly also because I have been in the country for quite a while now and understand the language better, especially the local accent. The work itself is also more pleasant since there is no piecework. This allows for more time for a chat (or two) with colleagues.

I familiarise myself with the surrounding area and memorise the storage locations of the various items. I, too, receive a certain number of orders every morning, have to pick the respective items from the various shelves according to size, colour, and shape, pack them at my table and label the boxes with the item numbers and quantities. The various parts of an order (only very few consist of only one box) are tied together and then sent with a copy of the order sheet for dispatch.

I am getting to know my new colleagues and the warehouse better. The work starts to be fun and the people are friendly and helpful. The young colleagues, in particular, talk to me often now and want to learn some German. Every word is greeted with astonishment. They try to repeat it but only get half of it. Nobody here speaks German, let alone any other foreign language.

I am amazed at how quickly I'm accepted here. After just a few weeks, I'm fully part of the team, complete my workload, and know my way around the warehouse. The items I deal with range from shirts, jackets, sweaters, gloves, and scarves to swimsuits, underwear and women's dresses.

Along with Bill, Glen also works at my packing table. He is a real original. I estimate his age to be in his mid-fifties. Glen has been with this company for forty years, and even his father used to work here. Back then, he tells me, there were many machines in this hall and production was still going on here. Unfortunately, only goods that are manufactured elsewhere are now stored in these halls. Many textiles come from Italy and the Far East. When you hear him talk like this, you can sense a kind of longing for a bygone era in his voice. The good old days. Everything was different back then. I like Glen and talk to him often. During the next few months, he will be the colleague I trust the most, and who I can always rely on.

Glen works to my right, and Bill to my left. Bill has also worked for this company for a long time, and has already retired, but occasionally helps out in the warehouse for a few weeks when things get busy, like now. He was a soldier in North Africa during World War II and was there when the Allies landed in Italy. However, he is never unfriendly to me, a young German. The war is long over, he says, making no distinction between me and the English young people. I like talking to him. He's a calm, kind, elderly man.

Dave works across from me. He is eighteen years old and has been working here for quite some time. I don't understand why he has no ambition to further his education because only those who qualify will find a better job later. He does this work for the money, he says. "You don't earn anything at school." I often find this attitude among my young colleagues. In the short term, they may be right. With the money they are earning, they can afford things that their peers, who are still at school, cannot afford. However, in the long term, they are ruining their future, because later on they have to work as unskilled workers for the same low wages as they do now. Then it's too late to change track and such people can hardly catch up.

Michele, a young girl who often draws during breaks, works at the second packing table. Her designs are really good. She would like to be an artist one day and by working here she earns part of the money she requires for her education. I like that attitude.

Joan works next to her. She is around forty years old, always funny, and laughs a lot.

Brian has his workplace opposite them. He's also very young, around twenty years old. He, too, would rather earn money than go to school.

John sits at the third packing table and writes shipping documents all day. The job is pretty monotonous and certainly boring. John is a bit odd. Now and then he sings, lets out shrill screams, and pretends to be "Rambo". However, when he's normal, he is actually quite nice.

Karl, twenty years old, works alongside John. I also talk to him very often. From time to time we stand in the narrow aisles with our packed items under our arms and chat. We have to be careful that no supervisor discovers us because sometimes one of them walks through the corridors and shows up completely unexpectedly. We've been caught chatting a few times instead of working. On such occasions, we always have a few packed items under our arms and then pretend to outsource or store something. Karl is a nice bloke. Unfortunately, he often goes to pubs, drinks a lot, and is sometimes late for work in the morning. He owned a fancy sports car, he tells me, a very nice vehicle. One evening, he crashed it while drunk. Karl has to be careful not to ruin his life.

There are also colleagues from distribution, other packers and supervisors, and I am slowly getting to know them all.

May 1985. Today, on the first of May, Marie will arrive. We haven't seen each other for seven weeks, it has been that long since I left Osnabrück. Last night, she took the night boat from the Hook of Holland to Harwich and from there, the train to Nottingham. She will arrive in Nottingham at around 1.30 p.m. I was given unpaid leave to pick her up, and I took the bus to Nottingham and got to the station on time.

The train pulls in, and a few minutes later we are reunited. When we hug, I realize how long seven weeks are, and how much I missed holding my wife in my arms. We're together again, if only for four days this time. We sit down on a bench on the square in front of the town hall, the sun is shining, and it's pleasantly warm. The impressive Nottingham Town Hall towers before us, two fountains splash on the square, and people stroll around or rest on benches like us. I tell my wife how things have been for me during the last few weeks. Above all, she is very excited to see the flat.

We take the bus to Derby, change at the central bus station, and continue to Duffield. We are very lucky with the weather. Under a brilliant blue sky, the surroundings of our new home appear even more beautiful than usual. Everything is completely new to Marie at the moment like it was to me seven weeks ago: the left-hand traffic, the language, the landscape, the construction of the houses. I have become used to all of this.

In Duffield, we walk up the lane to our flat. In the front gardens of the pretty cottages, the most beautiful flowers bloom now that spring has fully arrived. Marie is very taken with the rural idyll. If she also likes the flat, then everything is perfect.

We reach the house. It doesn't look particularly appealing from the front, but that does not matter. It is important that one feels comfortable inside. I unlock the front door and we take the stairs to the first floor. I guide Marie directly into the large living room with the wide bay window overlooking the garden. For me, it was love at first sight. Will she feel the same way? She does! She is just as excited about this room as I am. I then show her the other rooms. Everything is freshly painted, and the damage to the walls has been repaired. There are still a few things that need to be improved, for example, the carpet. Its colour is a dirty pink in the small room, a worn brown in the hallway, and in the kitchen the flooring is made up of several leftover pieces. This would have to be altered, but should not pose a problem in the medium term. The old gas stove in the kitchen has unsightly singed spots and the landlady has already indicated that the old device will be replaced by a newer electric stove.

During the next few days, Marie gets used to the flat. She also loves the surrounding area. Since I work during the day, she spends the time with Irene. I enjoy coming home from work in the evening and not being alone. Some normality is returning. On Saturday, we take the bus to Matlock, stroll through the streets, and look at the window displays.

The next day, it is already time to say goodbye again. However, this time it is only for five weeks because at the beginning of June, I plan to return to Osnabrück for a few days to fetch the car. In Nottingham, we have time to eat something, and then Marie's train pulls away towards the coast and I am alone again. Sentimentality arises, and a touch of sadness cannot be denied. I pull myself together. There is a lot to be done. I need to improve the flat and become acquainted with the new job.

I get along well at work and am accepted by my colleagues. Since nobody speaks German, I have to speak English all day long. This is how I learned many new words and entire phrases, becoming more confident every day. If I pick up an unfamiliar expression, I immediately ask Glen or Bill, who patiently explains it to me. I am very grateful for that. Every day I expand my vocabulary.

There is a ten-minute break in the morning and afternoon. Although officially, it is ten minutes, in reality, these breaks last much longer, sometimes almost twenty minutes. From time to time, even twenty-five to thirty minutes are reached. During the breaks, we read the newspaper, and Glen listens to the radio when a cricket match is being broadcast. He is crazy about cricket, although I honestly have no idea how this sport works. After the break, we slowly resume our work.

At first, I was surprised by the length of the breaks, but you can get used to anything. Of course, this won't last long as the excessive length of our breaks is noticed.

One day, a supervisor appears unexpectedly in our remote corner of the warehouse and finds us relaxing instead of working. He remarks pointedly, with an unmistakably sharp undertone, that the length of the break is supposed to be ten minutes and that we are probably overdoing it here. He has noticed this for quite a while. The complaint does not fail to have its effect. We push our sandwiches aside, fold the newspaper, turn down the radio, and get back to work.

For a few days, the breaks are really only ten minutes long and the supervisor keeps an eye on the situation. At first, he appears more often, then less regularly, and – after a week or two – the breaks become longer again, as less frequent checks are made. First, the ten minutes expand to fifteen, then the twenty-minute mark is tackled. My colleagues are slowly working their way up to the thirty-minute limit again, including me, of course, in solidarity. After a short period, we succeed. The supervisor has probably given up for the time being. The breaks again are thirty minutes long, we take our time and treat ourselves to some rest until the next reproval. Then, the whole process starts again.

My earnings have slightly increased, but at £45 gross per week (around £35 net), I am not among the top earners in the country. Every Friday morning is "payday" and that's when we get our wage packet. The content is no surprise, as we receive the same amount every week. I usually go shopping in the nearby supermarket in the evening, and half the money is gone by then. With the other half, I cover a part of the rental costs. Nothing more can be done with this weekly wage. For special expenses, I need to withdraw money from my bank account. However, I try to avoid this as far as possible and aim to get by with my current income.

When buying groceries, this means always choosing the cheapest products and abstaining from many things. At the moment, I am doing this out of pure ambition, as I want to know if it is feasible. While I could easily withdraw additional money if I wanted to, some people really have so little money at their disposal and have to get along with it. They can hardly afford anything and have to turn every penny over twice. I find this sad because now I know from my own experience how difficult it is to manage with such a low income.

In the evening, I walk home. In May the weather is fine, and I find the way home extremely relaxing.

Work ends at 5 p.m. I leave the factory premises and walk a short distance along the main road. At the end of town, I turn right, cross the Derwent on a steel bridge, and follow a narrow footpath that traces the river bank. On a sunny day, the bridge offers a great view across the dark waters of the sluggishly flowing river and I especially like the footpath along the shore. Shrubs, trees, dark water, pleasant warmth, everything is sprouting and blooming, and smells of spring. Further ahead, the river bends, and I follow a narrow country road over a wooded hill. At the top of the climb, I turn and look back at Belper. What a magnificent view! In front of me, the dark band of the Derwent runs through the green landscape, the banks lined with trees and hedges, and behind them the houses nestled in rolling hills. At this point, I am about halfway through. Just before Milford, the road crosses the railway line. A few meters from the bridge, the rails disappear in a tunnel. I often stop there and wait for the intercity train from London, which passes here every day around 5.30 p.m. If I am late, the waggons pass by on the other side of the meadow to my left. However, if I reach the bridge in time, the roar of the diesel engines can already be heard. A little later, the train shoots out of the tunnel and pulls away under me towards the north. At Milford, the country road joins the main route to Derby. I walk the last kilometre to Duffield beside the busy road and pass a farm with cows, horses, and sheep grazing on the surrounding pastures. In Duffield, I turn right, climb Castle Hill, turn onto Vicarage Lane, and arrive at my destination.

The house I live in is called "The Crows Nest" which fits perfectly because I feel very comfortable and secure within its walls, just like a bird in a nest. The name of the house could not be more appropriate.

During the following weeks, I will continue to renovate the flat. Irene gave me a leftover piece of fitted carpet for the corridor, and this is the first fitted carpet that I lay. Cutting the ends straight with a sharp Stanley knife is not that easy. The first attempts fail, and the material frays. However, I improve my cutting technique and, in the end, the final result is quite presentable. For the kitchen, I decide on a different solution. I have spotted self-adhesive linoleum tiles at a building centre that would fit well and are easy to install. As a colour combination, I chose white and blue, the colours of Bavaria (there has to be some connection to home). Every week, I buy eight white and eight blue tiles, which makes a total of sixteen tiles a week. After four weeks, the kitchen is finished and I am very satisfied with the result.

At work, my colleagues are starting to give me nicknames. As a German, you quickly become a "Kraut" in Britain. Some call me "Fritzi", which I don't mind. However, I find "Adolf" somewhat inappropriate as a colleague uses the name to allude to a specific epoch in German history. Calling me "Adolf" is not only distasteful to me, but also to some of my colleagues, and fortunately, it stops very quickly.

One day, I would have liked to use a phone card during the lunch break, but the card did not work. Although units are debited, the call is not connected. This is frustrating! I return to my workplace and vent my anger. However, I shouldn't have done this, because some colleagues seem to feel that their national pride has been offended. It is not that I criticised the technology of my host country, for heaven's sake, no! I would never come up with such a crazy idea. I am just angry because I lost money and couldn't make a phone call. In any other country, even my own, I would have reacted the same way. However, unfortunately, I have to say that quite a few Britons seem to have an extremely sensitive national feeling and therefore immediately perceive criticism of their country's technical achievements, among others, as criticism of their nation. British national pride is sometimes a bit strange. After three months in the country, this is becoming increasingly clear to me. The British are allowed to make fun of anything and criticise other nations. However, should a foreigner criticise something in their country, he receives a punishing look, a cold shoulder, and the instruction "not to be so arrogant". I therefore think it is highly advisable to immediately stop any criticism, as I am surprised at the irritated reaction of my colleagues. As a result, I do not criticise anymore and my colleagues calm down again. They have their national pride, and I have my peace. Another lesson learned.

Saturday, June 8th. I have been in the UK for three months, have been living in my flat for two months, and have been working at my second job for six weeks now. Today, I will return to Germany for seven days to help organise the upcoming furniture removal and to transport our car to Britain. Irene and John will also travel to Osnabrück at the same time to visit their son Peter, who is doing a work placement there. While they travel by plane, I take the train. They drop me off at Derby train station and continue to the East Midlands airport. My train leaves Derby at 8 a.m. I have to change trains in Leicester, reach the coast at Harwich, and take the ferry to Holland.

The weather is good, the sun is shining, clouds are appearing inland, and the sky is bright blue over the sea. The huge ferry slowly starts to move and leaves the harbour. We gradually reach our cruising speed, and the coast begins to fade in the distance. I sunbathe on the upper deck, keen not to miss the moment when the English coast disappears on the horizon. However, in the end, I miss it. When I get up and look back, we are only surrounded by water. The crossing will take eight hours. I take a stroll through the duty-free shop, eat something in the cafeteria, and study the cinema program. I find a film that interests me and so I spend the next two hours in the cinema on board. Afterwards, I return to the deck and rest in the sun for a while.

The Dutch coast appears and its contours quickly become clearer until we pass the dunes next to the harbour entrance of the Hook of Holland. I stand at the railing and watch the docking manoeuvre. From up here, I can see far into the distance and stay until most of the passengers have disembarked. Why should I join the long queue of people waiting and allow myself to be pushed towards the exit? I prefer to enjoy the glorious evening sun for a while and the view of the hustle and bustle below me on the quay.

Then, I also leave the ferry and go through customs. In which direction is it best to look? If you look directly at the customs officers, you will be checked. If you look away, you will also be checked. Whatever you do, it is wrong. I have to open my luggage. But, since I have nothing to hide, the customs officers don't find anything either.

Immediately after customs clearance, I go to the train station and board the train with the destination Berlin, which stops in

Osnabrück. It doesn't take long before the train leaves. We are well on time, and I should reach Osnabrück at around 11 p.m. as planned. However, after only ten minutes we suddenly stopped in the middle of nowhere and stayed there for over an hour. The conductor informs us that the electric locomotive had broken down and had to be towed away. "We're waiting for a replacement locomotive", he says. Finally, we continued, unfortunately, more than one hour late. Instead of 11 p.m., I shall thus arrive shortly after midnight.

Then, I am finally back at the railway station where my journey began thirteen weeks ago. Marie picks me up. What a strange feeling to be back in the place I left not so long ago, but which seems so far away due to the many new impressions and experiences of the last few weeks. Memories reawaken - I lived in Osnabrück for over a year - but I don't regret the decision to set off and leave the familiar. It is nice to be back, but I am already looking forward to returning to my new home. However, until then, there is a lot to be done. Furniture has to be dismantled and packed up, and books, dishes, and other belongings have to be wrapped up as well.

Sunday, June 9th. In the afternoon, we meet with Irene, John, and their son Peter. We pick them up from the hotel and drive to our flat because I want to show them how we lived in Germany. In the evening, we invite them to a restaurant in the old town of Osnabrück to say thank you for their great support during the last few months. They helped me to gain a foothold in their country, and I thank them by extending this invitation to a meal in my country.

Now, it's time to pack up our personal belongings. The furniture that we want to take with us has to be disassembled, while the rest is sold. It would be far too expensive to take everything to Britain. Many people respond to our newspaper advertisement, while the items that nobody wants go to bulky waste.

We plan our move as follows: an English transport company that moves the personal belongings of British soldiers to and from Osnabrück will deliver our furniture to Duffield at a reasonable price. Naturally, we also asked German transport companies for a quote. However, their prices were significantly higher than those of the British. We pay 1,200 D-Mark for the transport from flat to flat, including customs duties.

The first problem arises when we fill in the packing list as the dimensions of the pieces of furniture should be specified in inches, which doesn't mean very much to me at the moment. Therefore, I decide to state the dimensions in metric.

Our indoor plants are also a problem. Since some of the continental plant diseases are not found in Britain and are not wanted there either, no plants may be imported. We learn this from an English friend. After the initial disappointment, we made detailed enquiries at the plant protection office and we learned that five indoor plants may be imported. To do this, we would need a certificate from the plant protection office stating that the plants do not have any diseases. And that's exactly what we do. We have our plants checked and finally received the certificate. Hence, this problem is also solved.

On the way back by car, I'll already take some fragile items with me, especially our wedding crockery, to avoid any damage during transport. The five plants that we can take with us (thanks to the certificate) are also loaded into the car as they would certainly not survive the journey inside a dark furniture van for several days.

On Thursday evening, the car is fully loaded, and I'm ready to go. My very last evening in Osnabrück. Since I intend to leave tomorrow at 5 a.m., I set the alarm clock for 4.30 a.m.

Then, it is time to say goodbye again, although this time it will only be three weeks until Marie finally moves to Britain. Compared to the time we've already been apart, this is not long. We're almost there.

Friday, June 14th. I start the engine, Marie stands at the window and waves. One last look, then I'm on my way. It dawns when I leave Osnabrück and turn onto the motorway.

At the Dutch border, all papers for inspection are ready to hand, the certificate from the plant protection office, the rental agreement, and the certificate of employment. You never know what is checked at borders. However, all the excitement was for nothing. I pass the German-Dutch border without any problems, and nobody wants to see any papers. What I'm carrying in the car doesn't interest any of the customs officers. I really had not imagined it to be that easy. If I could now also enter the UK without any problems, everything would be perfect.

In the Netherlands, I am able to make good progress on the motorway. The ferry will leave the Hook of Holland at noon. So far, I'm on time and reach the port half an hour before the scheduled departure, where I join the long queue of waiting vehicles to board the ferry. Again, I have all the papers handy, and again, no one cares. Only my identity card is briefly looked at before I am waved through. Other vehicles pull up next to and behind me. Everyone is waiting to be allowed to enter the huge ferry. After a while, it finally starts, and my tyres also roll on board. I am instructed to approach the car in front of me as closely as possible, which I try to do without touching it. I turn off the engine, get out, and go up a steel staircase to the upper decks.

The ferry begins to fill with people and I rush to get a seat by the window. There are still enough places available, but this will change quickly. The armchairs with their high backrests are upholstered, which is pleasant. I sat behind the steering wheel for seven hours and realized that I was very tired. Therefore, I'm happy that I can rest now for the next five hours, which is how long the crossing to Harwich will take.

We cast off. Our giant ferry slowly pushes past the dunes towards the sea. In the calm waters of the port area, the ship only sways slightly. But, when we reach the open sea, the journey becomes more rough and white foam crowns dance in front of the window. The ship is now rolling through the water, and the fluctuations can be clearly felt. Suddenly, I think about my car deep down inside the ship. Is the handbrake on tight enough? I have to think about how close the vehicles are and the serious damage that could result if my car isn't properly secured.

I decide to go down to the parking spaces again to see if the handbrake is really sufficiently tightened. However, this is easier said than done. I descend the steel stairs but find the door to the vehicle decks locked. What now? If I can't make sure that everything is in order with my car, I am sure I won't have a relaxed crossing. I return to the deck, talk to the first person I see in a ship's uniform and explain my problem. I am lucky, the man is very helpful. We climb down together, he unlocks the door, and I go to my vehicle and check the handbrake. It is tight. Now I can enjoy the trip with peace of mind.

At around 6 p.m. English time, we enter the port of Harwich. The weather is fine, the sun is shining, and Great Britain welcomes me from its most beautiful side.

I go to my car, sit behind the steering wheel, and wait until the exit of the ferry slowly opens and I can drive ashore.

There are no problems with passport control.

Customs clearance follows and I am curious to see what will happen now, especially with regard to the plants that have been brought along. In any case, the necessary papers are ready to hand next to me. In fact, everything should be fine. Should be! However, things turn out a bit differently.

One of the customs officers signals me to pull over. I comply, open the side window, and show him all the documents that I am carrying with me for this specific case. However, these papers do not seem to interest him at all. He wants to see my driving licence plus the "green insurance card" for foreign citizens. Unfortunately, I do not have this particular insurance card! Although I have been everywhere to get documents, I had not thought of the green insurance card. And that's exactly what the customs officer wants to see now. Bad luck! "But how about certificates from the plant protection office?" I try humour, but without success.

He asks me to get out of the car and follow him. I do this and meet a senior officer. The man is polite, which makes things easier. He notified me that since my current residence is in the UK, I am practically importing my car into the country. Therefore, the vehicle is subject to special customs regulations for one year. If I sell it in the UK within the first year, I shall have to declare this to customs and pay tax. I am surprised at this, as I had not thought of it. I need to fill in a form and provide information about the vehicle. Unfortunately, this import issue is not the only problem, and the next challenges arise immediately after the first was dealt with. I have to prove that my car is properly insured in Great Britain, which I, unfortunately, cannot do. The officer tells me that I can't continue if the car isn't legally insured in the UK and proposes the following solution: the office of the British Automobile Club is just around the corner. There, I can have my vehicle insured with a British insurance company, which I have to do anyway if I want to stay in the country for a longer time.

Thus, I enter the office of the automobile club and explain my problem. Forms have to be filled in again. A computer is fed with my data, and the answer takes a little longer. Finally, there is a result. The cheapest insurance for my vehicle is £54 per year, based on a period of six accident-free years. Now for the payment. "Is this amount to be paid immediately, or can I transfer the money in a few days?" "Immediately, here and now," is the answer. Where there is one problem, there are certainly two. I don't have that much money with me and my chequebook is at home. Fantastic! What now? The problem can still be solved. The car is insured in the UK from tonight provided I transfer the £54 payment within the next seven days or the insurance will expire.

I finally got the document that I had to present to the customs officer so that I could enter the country with the vehicle.

No customs officer wanted to see the papers I had with me, no one was remotely interested in the five indoor plants. What I don't have, is what they wanted to see. "C'est la vie", that's the way it is in life.

I leave the port and have to concentrate on the left-hand traffic. For the first time in my life, I am driving a car on the left side of the road. What a challenge, especially with a vehicle in which the driver's seat is on the left! At first, it feels strange. While going straight is easy, turning at road junctions and changing directions can be really dangerous if you're not always fully concentrated. I must not drive like I am used to, as this could have fatal consequences.

Luckily, after I leave Harwich, the road runs across the countryside rather than through towns and villages. Notices in three languages remind drivers that they have to drive on the left side in this country.

It's a sunny evening with little traffic on the road. I feel fit and rested. Unfortunately, I lost more than one hour due to customs formalities, and could already have been a lot further along my journey.

I reach Colchester where my brief driving experience in left-hand traffic is seriously tested for the first time. Suddenly, there is a lot of oncoming traffic, pedestrians appear, and cyclists overtake me or have to be overtaken. The road runs right through the town. I have to concentrate on the signposts to not lose my way, watch out for oncoming traffic, and always keep to the left, while the temptation to intuitively pull over to the right persists. I feel insecure! Sometimes, there are direction signs at one junction, then they are missing at another one. I often have to make quick decisions, turn off, and drive around in circles. Finally, I managed to leave Colchester and even end up on the right road. The first acid test in left-hand traffic has been passed.

At Bishop's Stortford, I join the M11 motorway, and the journey becomes easier as there are no more towns to drive through on the three-lane motorway. At Cambridge, the M11 joins the dual carriageway A1. It's starting to get dark and I still have a long way to go to Grantham and from there, via Nottingham, to Derby. I take a break, rest, and then drive on.

Around midnight, I am still driving north on the A1 and reach Grantham at 1 a.m. According to the map, I have to turn off here in the direction of Nottingham, and I pay careful attention to the road signs but cannot find indications, and start to get nervous. Finally, Nottingham is displayed. I leave the A1 and drive west. After passing Nottingham, I am back in familiar surroundings, find my way without any problems, reach Duffield, and turn into our lane.

It's almost three o'clock in the morning and already starting to get light. I park the car and leave everything in it - I will unpack later. Dead tired, all I want to do is slip into my sleeping bag and rest. After one week in Germany, I'm back in my little flat in the heart of England, in front of the huge chestnut tree. The return journey took around twenty-two hours. As soon as I lay down on the mattress, I fell asleep.

After seven hours, the noise of the day wakes me up. Today I have to go shopping because there is almost nothing left to eat. First, however, I unpack the car. The plants survived the journey well, and the wedding crockery did not break. Our first belongings are now in the country. The flat was nearly empty and now, for the first time, boxes, plants and pieces of furniture fill the rooms. How beautiful the flat will look after we've furnished it comfortably with our remaining furniture in a few weeks.

The following two weeks pass very quickly. I bought some chocolate in Germany as a gift for my colleagues, assuming it would be something special. Later I find the same chocolate in a local supermarket. However, my colleagues are very happy about the small gift.

Sunday, June 23rd. It is raining and I stay at home and read. In the evening, the rain subsides and some rays of sunshine appear. I decide to go out into the fresh air, walk through nature, and think. I've been in Britain for four months now and we intend to stay for two years.

Suddenly, a certain feeling of insecurity returns. During the first few days, I was worried about not finding a flat. Then came the fear of not being able to find a job. Now this feeling of doubt gets hold of me for the third time. Are we financially able to stay in the UK? Will we succeed or fail? What if it goes wrong? Until now we still had the flat in Germany, and a return would have been possible. However, once the move is complete, there's no turning back, at least for the next two years. Have I been able to consolidate the basis over the last four months to such an extent that our ambitious foreign project can be a success?

The weather is changing. Dark clouds are approaching from the west, and the wind is picking up. The poor weather conditions reinforce my feeling of insecurity. Can we realize our plan? We just have to succeed, there's no turning back. I have to suppress the negative thoughts for the third time. Now don't panic! Not after everything I've already achieved. However, this is not easy. How will the return to Germany work, later, in a few years? Many questions run through my head. I try to analyse the situation logically and calmly. We have made our decision. So far, everything has gone well, but there is still a lot to do. Time will tell. Two years is not forever. We will find solutions as we have always been able to.

During the next few days, I receive replies to written applications. Unfortunately, all of them are negative. Luckily I have a job in the textile company.

Another reply letter gives hope. I had also applied to a college in Derby to test the possibility of teaching German and the headmaster invited me for an interview. During this conversation, I learned that I currently do not meet the requirements to be able to teach because I am not a trained teacher. However, there is a training course for those interested in working in adult education. This so-called Stage One Training Course lasts three months, takes place once a week in the evening, and concludes with a certificate. After successful completion, I can teach to a limited extent. The headmaster even hints at the possibility that I might be able to supervise a German conversation class during the training course. Sounds good! I'm excited. However, he unfortunately cannot tell me anything specific at the moment. If I am interested in participating in this course, which starts at the end of September, I have to register in writing. He gives me the address. This conversation raises my morale. Something is happening. My confidence is returning, my ambition is unbroken.

I write to the Derby County Council and sign up. If you have a plan and look positively into the future, then there is no time for negative thoughts. Attacking is the best form of defence.

One week before Marie's arrival, I spot a job advertisement that exactly matches her education and previous professional career. Such qualified advertisements are rare. A textile company is looking for a secretary for the export manager. Fluent language skills in German and French, as well as several years of professional experience in a similar position, are required. So, what to do? Marie won't be here for a week. By then it could be too late. You can't let an opportunity like this pass. After careful consideration, I decided to help luck a bit, write a letter of application in her name, and post it the same day. Let's see what happens. In the event of a positive answer, I'm sure I'll come up with something in due course.

The last weekend in June is the last weekend on my own. On Wednesday, July 3rd, my wife will also move to Britain. After her last working day in Osnabrück, she will take the overnight ferry from the Hook of Holland to Harwich on Tuesday evening and from there the train to Nottingham. Since I have to work on Wednesday and have asked for unpaid leave too many times, Irene agrees to pick her up in Nottingham. The last few days of being alone passed more quickly than expected.

I had almost forgotten the application I sent in Marie's name when one morning I found a letter in the mailbox inviting her to an interview on Friday, July 5th. That would be exactly two days after Marie's arrival! Now I have to think of something very quickly.

July 1985. I return home from work on Wednesday 3rd, knowing I won't find an empty flat tonight because my wife will be there. Finally, we are reunited. I left the front door key with the neighbours this morning so that Marie can enter the flat in the afternoon. As always, I park the car behind the house right under the chestnut tree and look up at our flat. One of the sliding windows in the living room is open, Marie's head appears, and she smiles. We are both happy that the four-month separation is over. The first and most difficult time of our foreign project has been successfully completed.

That evening I confessed about the application letter on her behalf and the invitation to the interview in just two days. Marie is surprised but decides to attend the interview. It's an opportunity.

Friday, July 5th. I drive Marie to a small village about thirty minutes north-east of Derby. The company that invited her for an interview has its headquarters there. We arrive at 8 a.m., although the appointment isn't until 9 a.m. However, I have to return to Belper because my work starts at 8.30 a.m.

When I see Marie standing all by herself in the empty car park in front of the office building, I am very proud of her. Only two days in Britain and she has to find her way here all by herself. I know that she'll be just as dedicated as I would have been.

In the evening I am very curious to find out how the interview went. Marie tells me that she spoke to the secretary of the export manager who is currently in Australia on business. She had to write some texts in English, German, and French shorthand, translate a few sentences and answer questions about her education and work experience. As far as her language skills in German and French are concerned, she fully met the desired requirements. Concerning the English language, of course, she does not yet have the required routine and experience. They both saw it that way and agreed that it would be better to start with an easier job during the first few months to get used to the English language and build up fluency. Despite this decision, the company kept her records. If a suitable position needs to be filled in the near future, she will be notified.

Of course, we are disappointed that it didn't work out in the end, although this position would have been too high for a first job abroad. It was an opportunity and we tried.

I am proud of my wife. Despite the short-term appointment, she didn't back down. For that reason alone, it was a great personal success.

We spend our first weekend together without furniture. While we were told that the transport could take up to two weeks, we do not know how long it really will take. We have the phone number of the transport company. If our furniture still hasn't arrived after two weeks, we should call them.

One week goes by without a trace of our furniture. Our impatience grows! Sleeping on a mattress on the floor takes some getting used to and we'd love to set up our furniture.

I call the transport company the following Monday. The furniture is already in the country, but customs clearance could take a few more days, I am told. I hope it's only a few days! But, getting impatient is useless. We can only wait and see. Days go by, and the furniture doesn't arrive. Our patience is being put to the test. Again, I call and again I am assured that it could only be a matter of a few days.

Marie starts looking for a job. She adopts the same strategy I did, namely visiting companies and asking for work on the spot. First, she tackles the department stores, supermarkets, and retail outlets in Derby. Unfortunately, without success. Then, she visits employment agencies to register there, and hands in her CV plus copies of certificates.

During this week, she is always very exhausted in the evening and sometimes just as frustrated as I was during my first week in the UK. But there is always a new day, new hope, new opportunities. Success could come tomorrow, who knows?

A surprise awaits us on Saturday. The company where John works is looking for a temporary worker for the canteen for six weeks and Marie could work there if she wanted to. This is exactly what we need now. As we learn about the weekly earnings, this day just keeps getting better. Marie would be paid £62 a week. In comparison, I currently earn only £45 per week. She accepts the job offer. With our combined earnings, we now have a weekly gross income of £107. What a success! We are now earning enough to be able to support ourselves in the UK just from the income we generate in the country, and we do not have to rely on our savings any more. One of our goals has thus been achieved. We dared to do something special and are on the road to success.

Monday, July 15th. Marie starts working in a factory canteen just two weeks after her arrival. Everything would be perfect if only our furniture would finally arrive. Where is it? Why is this taking so long? The days go by, and no furniture arrives.

Friday, July 19th. We shop in the evening. When we get home around 6.30 p.m., we cannot believe our eyes. A furniture lorry is parked in front of the house. Our furniture! We finally received our furniture and can set up the flat.

When the lorry is opened, we are quite shocked at the disorder that reigns inside. We learn that there are two deliveries on this furniture lorry. One is ours, and the other will go on to Scotland. Furniture, crates, boxes, and two folding boats above them are in the loading area. Hopefully, we can find all our pieces in this chaos. The removal men are friendly and help us carry our belongings upstairs. We are amazed at how quickly this is done. In no time at all, our belongings are upstairs in the flat.

When the men left, we stood between our furniture and still could not quite believe that we finally had everything. How familiar a strange place suddenly appears when you have your own belongings. A new flat becomes a home, wherever that may be. Finally, we can start to set up our new home. For me, four months of camping on a mattress on the floor is coming to an end that evening. We set up our bed first because neither of us wanted to spend another night on the floor. Luxury is slowly returning to our lives.

During the next few days, we encounter some problems in setting up our new home. We cannot connect any of our electrical devices as the plugs do not fit UK sockets. The voltage in Britain is also higher than in Germany, instead of 220 volts it is 240 volts here. What to do?

John finds a solution. He disconnects the German plugs and fits British plugs onto the appliances. However, how do we deal with the higher voltage? Can we connect our devices? I am particularly worried about the stereo, which I really don't want to ruin. Luckily, John is a keen technician. No problem is too difficult for him, and nothing is unsolvable. He orders a small transformer that reduces 240 volts to 220 volts and the refrigerator and stereo system are connected to the transformer.

We don't use the washing machine, because we would require a stronger transformer for it which would be much too expensive - we could almost buy a new washing machine for that price. Therefore, we use a laundry service once a week which not only is relatively inexpensive but also very convenient.

Step by step, we assemble our furniture, and the flat starts becoming comfortable. The small room becomes our dining room as it is unsuitable as a bedroom due to the TV set in the flat below plus the lack of heating during the cold season. We set up the large room as a combined living and bedroom and placed our double bed directly opposite the large bay window. The commode fits next to the fireplace, a wooden shelf also finds its place. What is missing now? A wardrobe and a desk. On a Saturday morning, we find what we are looking for in a furniture shop. The wardrobe fits next to the shelf, and the desk is placed in front of the bay window. From there, the view of the garden is fantastic! The room is bright, and we feel very comfortable. By the end of July, the flat was fully furnished and the voltage problems were solved.

Marie has been working in the factory canteen for a few weeks now. She enjoys the job, is doing fine, and can improve her language skills.

We both mastered the start of our professional life in a foreign country in a relatively short time with ordinary jobs. Later on, when we are confident in the foreign language, we can advance. At work, we learn new words and expressions every day, and we are fully immersed in the English language. We listen, speak, become more confident, and are lucky that none of our colleagues speaks our mother tongue. We have to communicate in English and that's exactly what we want.

I now drive to work in the car, but use the bicycle on sunny days. Marie takes the bus from Duffield to Darley Abbey and from there, John takes her in the car. It is a long trip for her, but she's happy to have a job.

Now it is time for us to register with a National Health Service doctor. In the local surgery, we can choose a doctor whose list we want to be on.

August 1985. We've settled in, the furniture has been set up, technical problems have been solved, and missing items have been bought. We are satisfied with our current jobs, get along well with our colleagues and become more confident in communicating in English. Our combined earnings are sufficient to finance our foreign project. Although we cannot make big leaps yet, at the end of the week we even have some money left over to go to the cinema or a small restaurant. We are convinced that moving to the UK was the right decision.

We cannot save anything at the moment because we need what we earn for everyday life, but we are happy with this investment in our future. In case of an emergency, there is a financial cushion in Germany.

We make friends, are invited out, and extend invitations to others. Life begins to normalize. Soon everything will be almost the same as in Osnabrück. The only difference is that we now speak English with our new friends instead of German or French.

We got used to driving on the left, albeit not without problems. Especially in the beginning, left-hand traffic was a source of danger that should not be underestimated. During the first few days – and even weeks – we always looked in the wrong direction before crossing a street. More than once, we were really lucky as we almost got under the wheels of an oncoming vehicle. Since then, we forced ourselves to look both ways before crossing a street. Better safe than sorry. I especially have to concentrate when driving. We still have the car from the Continent with the steering wheel on the left, which is problematic for left-hand traffic.

Our first visitor from the family is my brother. One evening, we receive a telegram in which he tells us that he is in London with his girlfriend and wants to stop by tomorrow. Since the information was written the day before according to the date, the two should show up today and it doesn't take long before they appear. Naturally, we are happy about this surprise. After their visit, they intend to continue their journey to Scotland. We spend a nice evening together and have a lot to tell each other. The next morning, I take them to Belper in the car and drop them off at the end of the town. While I go to work, they try to hitchhike. In two weeks, they plan to visit us again on their return journey.

On a Saturday at the end of August, we go down to London by coach. Intercity coaches are the cheapest form of transport in the UK. It is our first small holiday and we enjoy it. London has a very special flair with its unique red double-decker buses and black taxis. The parks provide a lot of greenery and one doesn't get the impression of being in a concrete jungle. When we return to Derby late in the evening we are pleased and feel rewarded for the efforts of the last few weeks and months.

Many students have holiday jobs during their semester break and some of them also work in our textile company. I like talking to them, as there are always interesting topics to discuss. One student even speaks some French.

This is how the weeks go by during the summer of 1985 in Derbyshire. There are a few hot days, but otherwise, the weather is rather mixed. We are content, have jobs, a nice flat, and are making new friends.

However, all of a sudden this quiet life is interrupted. Marie feels a lump in her breast and sees a doctor. He prescribes her medicine. Unfortunately, she discovers that she is allergic to penicillin, develops a rash, is ill for a week, cannot go to work, and does not receive any wages. This is what happens when you don't have a permanent contract of employment. After a week, she is better again. Although the rash is healed, the problem with the lump remains.

A few days later we talked to friends about it and they advised us to have the lump removed. But we are in a foreign country. Are we insured? We need to find out as soon as possible if Marie can have surgery in the UK. We enquire and receive the information that it is possible. As we both work in the UK and pay our contribution to the National Health System like any other employee, we are entitled to medical treatment and therefore to an operation. We also learned that we would even have to have the operation carried out in the UK since we are currently no longer insured in Germany.

An operation is never an easy decision. No one likes going into a hospital, especially in a foreign country with an unfamiliar system and a different language. However, we think it is safer to have the lump removed. On Monday, Marie sees the doctor again to arrange a hospital appointment. While there generally is rather a long waiting time for NHS surgeries, the lump in Marie's breast seems to worry the doctor as well. We are amazed to learn that Marie will be able to go to Derby City Hospital next Sunday already and be operated on the following Monday. We are both very happy about this.

Sunday, September 15th. I accompany Marie to the hospital. After registration, we are led to her ward. This is still in the old building complex, the new one is currently under construction. The ward is very long and holds many beds. I stay an hour before leaving, but promise to come back later.

In the evening, Marie is very composed. As I leave her, I feel anxious, like anyone who has to leave a family member in the hospital knowing that an operation will take place the next day.

It's the uncertainty. You can only wait and hope that everything goes well. One last look, she waves to me, and then I have to go. Hopefully, everything will be fine.

Monday, September 16th. The day of the operation. I find it difficult to concentrate at work. In the evening, I drive straight to the hospital. In what condition will I find my wife? I enter the ward and spot her sitting on the bed eating something. The operation went well, the lump was removed and is being examined in the laboratory. In a few days, we will be informed of the result.

We are glad that everything went well. The doctors and nurses are all very friendly, and an assistant doctor even speaks some French. In the evening I returned home feeling calmer than yesterday. Maybe Marie can leave the hospital tomorrow.

The next day, we learn that Marie really can go home and we are very happy about this although it would have been better if she could have stayed in the hospital for a few more days because now she is alone in the flat all day long. I have to work, as otherwise there is no money. Being alone leads to mild depression. Marie needs care and luckily Irene helps us. She comes to the flat the very next day and stays until the evening. Marie spends the following day with her at Darley Abbey. After that, she can manage on her own again.

A week later we received the result of the laboratory test. The lump is not malignant, and thus everything is fine. We are relieved.

THIRD JOB
AS A WAREHOUSE WORKER
IN A TEXTILE COMPANY

September brings a change. The summer months with the working students were interesting. But the current salary is modest, the semester break is over, and the students are returning to their colleges. Time to think about some changes in our situation. Since Marie's earnings are almost twice as high as mine, I should change something.

During the next few days, I consider the situation. We went abroad to risk something. I currently have a small, albeit regular income. But is this what I want? I decide to take a risk and look for a new job.

I resign on September 20th. Now, I am free to try something new. However, will I be able to find a better job quickly? There is no point in brooding. The adventure of another job search is waiting for me. It never took me long to find work in the UK. After a few hours of intense searching, I was always successful. I'm highly motivated and self-confident to walk from door to door again and look for a new job.

However, before I leave my current employer, I ask for a written job reference. This surprises him, as it does not seem to be a common request that temporary employees make. Nevertheless, I receive the reference. You never know what you will need such proof for.

Friday, September 20th. Today is my last workday at Belper. I am a bit sad when it is time to say goodbye to the colleagues with whom I've worked for five months. Real friendships have developed with some of them.

In the afternoon, I receive a parting gift. Each colleague contributed some money with which they bought me some wonderful leather gloves, which will be very useful for the next winter. I promise to stop by sometimes and tell them how I'm doing professionally.

That evening I left the company premises for the last time. Everything comes to an end at some point and it is always a risk to leave the familiar. In such moments, one must not only see what one gives up. Something else begins, a new adventure is already waiting, and that's exactly what I feel now. This chapter of my life is closed, and I decided it myself.

Monday, September 23rd. Today I can once again determine the future myself, which is very motivating. I feel free, courageous, and self-confident, but also a little nervous and tense. I know I have to knock on doors again. Nobody will help me, I have to do it all by myself. Will I find a new job today? Or tomorrow or the day after tomorrow? Where will I work and what will I do? All these questions are running through my head this morning.

I am too excited to eat much for breakfast. A piece of bread and a glass of milk, and then I set off. Marie is not working at the moment, as she has to recover from the operation. Hence, we currently have no income and everything now depends on how quickly I can find a new job. This doesn't bother me as the hunting instinct prevails. There are financial reserves for emergencies.

I get into the car and drive to the industrial estate in the south of the city of Derby. This third job hunt is more comfortable than the first two because I now have a car. During my first attempts,

I didn't even have a bicycle. Today, I am more mobile and have a greater reach.

After my arrival on the industrial estate, I take a look around first to find out which companies are based here. There are loads of them. It should be possible to find a job on this estate. I park the car and set off on foot. Where do I start? Which company do I visit first? The first attempt is always the hardest, one is still a bit nervous. After that, routine sets in and self-confidence prevails.

I start my job search with a company whose appearance I like most. The lady at reception is very friendly, I present my request, and she calls the HR department. Unfortunately, there are no vacancies. However, I should leave a copy of my CV, they want to check it and notify me in writing. This is not bad for a start as at least it's not a general rejection.

I visit all the companies in the area. These are small to medium-sized businesses from different sectors: a warehouse for electronic parts, a car dealer for a German luxury brand, a glass factory, a furniture store, a laundry, a tyre dealer, a shipping company, the logistics centre of a supermarket chain, a large bakery, various handicraft businesses and so on. It works well. I enter, present my request and wait for an answer regarding vacancies. If there are none, I try my luck with the next company. Since there are many businesses in this industrial estate and therefore potential prospects of success, I am highly motivated.

At the laundry, I get straight through to HR but, in the end, there is no job for me here either.

After I visited eleven companies without success, I felt slightly disappointed. This is a dangerous moment! Give up or keep going? Can I still motivate myself?

It's noon and I decide to take a break, buy a sandwich, get in the car and rest.

Afterwards, I look for work again.

A porter refuses me access to the warehouse of a furniture store. We start talking. He knows Germany, raves about beer, bratwurst, and wine and becomes really talkative. However, all the beautiful memories of his stay in my home country cannot convince him to let me pass. Job seekers have to apply in writing. There is nothing that can be done.

A few steps further is the logistics centre of a supermarket chain. A high fence blocks access and the guardhouse at the entrance is manned. There is definitely no getting through here either. I spoke to one of the security guards and received an address and a phone number. I should call there or send my written application. I take the information and continue searching.

It's already after 2 p.m. I've visited sixteen companies, sixteen times without success. Should I stop for today and continue tomorrow? My confidence is beginning to crumble, but I'm not thinking about giving up yet. I have nothing to lose. I decided to keep on searching, there are still enough companies left.

I come across a small building materials company. The secretary at reception asks me to take a seat. A forklift driver is currently being sought. Would that interest me? "Why not, what are the conditions?" She tells me that she has to talk to the boss about that but he isn't in the office at the moment and he will not be back for an hour. "Could you come back in an hour?"

That's how it is sometimes. I almost wanted to break off my search for today, and now there seems to be an opportunity. However, I don't know if I would even be suitable for this job, since you need a special license to drive a forklift, which I don't have. But I can get this license and the possible opportunity gives me an incredible boost.

I use this positive feeling to keep on searching. Maybe I'll even manage to find something else in the meantime. Waiting an hour would be a waste of time. If nothing can be found, I can always return and speak to the boss.

My mood improves and I visit a few more companies, albeit without success. Another half hour passes, and I cannot find a new job.

At the reception of a textile company, I ask about vacancies and expect a negative answer. I am momentarily surprised when this does not happen and I hear that employees are currently being sought for the warehouse. Some applicants have already appeared for interviews today. Should I be interested, I could join them.

Yes, I am interested! The woman at reception calls HR. Shortly thereafter, I am picked up and taken to the HR manager. Somehow I still cannot quite grasp the whole thing. Suddenly, everything seems so easy. I visited twenty-one companies today, and there weren't any real job offers. This is now the twenty-second company and they are actually looking for someone in a field in which I have already worked in this country for five months and have a reference. If that's not an advantage! However, I should better not get excited too soon.

We walk through a large factory hall where many women are sitting at tables and working at sewing machines, walk along a corridor, and reach the personnel office. The HR manager is very friendly, asks me to sit down, and wants to know where I'm from, how long I've been in the country, and where I've worked so far. Now the job reference from Belper is very valuable as it turns out that both textile companies belong to the same group of companies.

The HR manager seems impressed by my CV and informs me that the responsible supervisor will come around shortly to see me as well. It doesn't take long before she turns up, exchanges a few words with the HR manager, reads through my CV, takes a look at the job reference and asks me to follow her to the warehouse. It is bright and very clean here. Textiles of different sizes, shapes, and colours hang on two floors, neatly packed in plastic bags. I learned that the job entails the storage and removal of textiles, as well as putting together the daily deliveries. That would be roughly the same job as the one in Belper.

"How much can I earn here?" When the conversation turns to money, she hesitates. "Unfortunately, one doesn't earn very much in the textile industry", she begins tentatively. That doesn't sound very promising. So how much? "Only £75 a week", she explains.

Wages of £75 a week! Compared to the £35 net in Belper, that would more than double my weekly earnings. I am excited as I wouldn't have expected that much. The supervisor is surprised that someone can be so happy about so little money. She asks expectantly whether I want the job. Yes, of course I want it! "When can I start?" "Tomorrow morning at 8 o'clock." "Good, then see you tomorrow morning in the personnel office." There I would receive a clock card and have to fill in the employee form.

That's it for today. I have a new job. Again, I only needed one day, seven hours to be exact. I've visited more than twenty companies. It is my third job in the UK in seven months. During this time, I was able to increase my weekly income from £25 to £35 and now to £75 gross. This is still not a top income, but a nice personal success. The risk of giving up the job in Belper to look for something new has paid off.

I do not return to the company that is looking for a forklift driver. I found a new job, the income is satisfying for the moment, so why keep on searching?

That evening I did not immediately inform Marie about the good news, as I wanted a bit of excitement to build. When I finally told her about what happened today she was overjoyed. It is like a fairy tale. We feel infinitely rich this evening and would not want to swap places with anyone in the world at the moment. We are happy and proud. What a wonderful feeling to have achieved something on your own. This gives one a lot of self-confidence and one benefits from such an experience for life.

We enjoy the evening and celebrate the success at a small restaurant. There are enough reasons to celebrate: Marie's operation went well, the lump wasn't malignant, I successfully changed jobs and, on top of that, doubled my income.

Tuesday, September 24th. My first day at the new job. Instead of ten minutes to Belper, it now takes me around twenty-five minutes by car to get to my new workplace. My shift starts at 8 a.m. First of all, I received a clock card this morning. Everything is new to me here. I feel quite lost, don't know anyone, and the surroundings, products and premises are unfamiliar. However, everything new takes time. I so often had to get used to something new.

I spend the first day mainly getting to know my colleagues and the premises. The people who work here are almost all very young. About twenty people work in the warehouse, and many more in production. Finding the way around the warehouse and getting to know the new products also takes time. At my previous job, of course, I knew every corner. Here, I start again from scratch, have to be patient, and slowly get used to it.

This week, I also visited Derby College for the first time on Friday evening to attend the training course for new teachers for further education. Participation in this course results from a meeting with a headmaster in June. At that time, I enquired about the possibility of being able to teach German. Since I am not a trained teacher, participation in this course is mandatory. It is organised by the local authority, is free of charge and, if successful, concludes with the "Stage One Certificate". I signed up and was invited to participate. Now, at the end of September, the course starts, takes place on Fridays from 8 p.m. to 10 p.m. plus twice on Saturdays all day and runs for three months, i.e. until shortly before Christmas. There are ten people in the group.

Saturday, September 28th. Marie is going to visit her family in France for two weeks. She has recovered well from the surgery but still needs some rest. A visit to her parents will thus do her good. She takes a coach from Derby to Tours via London. These long-distance coaches are the cheapest way to travel, cheaper than taking the train, and also more convenient as one's luggage can stay on the coach when crossing the English Channel.

While Marie is in France, I won't get bored, because there is a lot to be done. I have to get used to my new job and the study group at the college.

It takes time to get by in the warehouse and to have an idea of where the various items are stored. This is important because in the future I will have to find the items quickly when compiling orders. On my second working day, I draw a plan of the premises with detailed information about items and their article numbers. There are many variants in different storage locations. I have to get used to everything.

Another warehouse worker starts on the job this week. Like me, he is also a temporary worker. "Temps" do not have a permanent employment contract, are hired if necessary and can be made redundant at short notice. As a "temp" you have almost no security.

My colleague's name is Trevor and he originates from Jamaica. Since we're both new and don't know anyone, we quickly become friends. He is a nice bloke, and we work together and help each other. We're both different from the others, and that unites us. I'm a foreigner with a different mother tongue, he's a native speaker (albeit with a heavy Caribbean accent), but his skin tone is dark. We stick together. This is a big help for me.

The level of education of some colleagues is not very high and it is almost normal that there is a lot of swearing and the jokes are quite rough. But, it's not too bad. I also learn new words every day, have them explained, and use them. The foreign language is always around me.

The daily work is very monotonous. In the morning, textiles that are lined up on long rails have to be wrapped up in plastic bags. These are orders that have already been put together and are now being prepared for transport. It is pretty hard physical work. The plastic cover is pulled over the garments from below, closed at the top and provided with a sticker. This requires bending down, pulling up, locking, bending down again, pulling up, and locking, all morning long. Luckily the radio is on. Music makes hard work feel a little easier.

Shortly before noon, a lorry pulls up and has to be loaded with the packaged items in the afternoon. Afterwards, we pick new orders, which are packed and loaded the next day. New textiles from production also have to be stored away.

Slowly, I get to know the individual items and their storage locations.

At noon we can eat in a canteen which offers turkey or lamb with chips, peas, carrots, mashed potatoes and sometimes pizza. I like it. Doing physical work throughout the day gives you a hearty appetite.

I visit the college every Friday night. I am the only foreigner in the "Stage One Training Course", but this doesn't bother me. On the contrary, it is very helpful for my English. I am also the only candidate who wants to teach a foreign language. The subjects of the other participants include aerobics, keep-fit, tap dancing, falconry, painting, the history of the Vikings, and much more. A wide range of interesting fields of knowledge. Like me, all participants are specialists in their fields but do not have any special training for teaching. The aim of this course is to convey information concerning the learning habits of adults. Not only expert knowledge is important, but also the way in which it is conveyed and how the lessons are made interesting for adults.

For me, these evenings are also an ideal opportunity to further improve my language skills. Compared to my colleagues at work, the people who are enrolled in the course are highly educated and it is very interesting to talk to them. We experience how adults learn, have to give lectures in front of the group, learn how to use technical devices, and much more. I like all of this and find that I look forward to Friday night all week. Here, I find a completely different milieu than at work. The job is important to earn money. However, apart from Trevor, I can hardly have a reasonable conversation with most of my colleagues as they just fool around.

The exciting aspect of my current life is the fact that I can actively determine the future myself. I can change things, gain experience, set goals and achieve them. I firmly believe in an interesting future, which I am now preparing for, and in which I shall certainly reap the rewards of my current efforts. I am completely satisfied with the state of my life at present.

Saturday, October 12th. Marie returns from France. In the evening, I pick her up from the Derby bus station. Despite the long drive, she looks relaxed and fit. The two weeks at home have obviously done her good.

On the way back to our flat, I tell her that a surprise is waiting for her at home which arouses her curiosity and she tries to find out what it is. However, I don't reveal anything, it's supposed to be a surprise. During the last two weeks, I decided to buy a small TV set. We had left our device in Germany because we were told that in Britain there are other transmission frequencies which would have rendered our old device useless. I lived without a TV set for seven months. While I don't regret it, I would also like to watch the news again. TV programmes not only provide information about the country and its people, but above all, you can hear the foreign language. We should use this opportunity. I saved £40 during the last two weeks and bought a small portable TV set. Marie had not expected this and she was delighted. Now we can discover the world of British television programmes, which are completely new to us. And, there are many new things to discover: new shows, faces, hosts, commercials and much more.

At the beginning of October, Marie also started looking for a new job because the post in the canteen was temporary. Although we knew this, it was a good start and we have not regretted it.

This time, when looking for employment, she can benefit again from connections through our friends. She is invited to an interview at the head office of the local building society. After the interview, she has to wait a few days for the result. During this time, she continues with her job search. The answer from the building society may be negative, so we have no time to lose.

One evening, she returns home happy and says that she found a job today entirely through her own initiative. She is very proud of this great personal success. She went to Belper by bus and visited the local chocolate factory. A few months ago, I also visited this factory, unfortunately without success. Marie was luckier today. Chocolate production for Christmas is in full swing. During a test, she had to do some work on the assembly line. The factory building is big and new, and inside it was hot and very noisy. At £75 gross a week, the work pays well but is limited to three months only. She must have passed the test to the satisfaction of the supervisor because she was offered the job and can start next Monday.

When I return home from work the next day, a surprise awaits me. This morning, Marie received a notification from the building society that she could get a part-time job in the office for three months if she was interested. The working time would be from 1 p.m. to 5 p.m. The weekly wage of £45 gross would be £30 below that of the chocolate factory, but the working conditions would be much better.

We have to make a decision. Everything was clear yesterday, there was only one job offer. That evening we went for a long walk and discussed the situation. In the fresh air, it is always easier to consider options, discuss situations, and make decisions. In the end, we decided on the part-time job offered by the building society. Although this is only a part-time post and therefore pays less, we secretly speculate that there might be another post after the three months. At the moment, however, this is pure speculation. We don't know if that could happen. But once you are employed by a company, the chances of being able to stay in case of internal job offers are certainly promising. After all, it is the head office of the local building society and there are certainly vacancies that are first advertised internally. Hence, we decided that Marie will accept the job offer that pays less at the moment but offers greater potential in the future. This actually turned out to be the right decision, but more on that later.

In October, Marie starts working at the building society. She can walk to her new workplace in around ten minutes. Both of our wages are now fully sufficient to finance our living expenses in Britain.

The weeks go by, and I've settled into my new job.

On a Friday afternoon in November, I have a verbal argument with a colleague. I was just putting together an order when he appeared and claimed that I criticised the quality of his work. This is true because he's generally perceived as layabout, not only by me but also from the perspective of my colleagues. He insults me and wants to unload his frustration on me. I keep on working but he's trying to provoke me further. Linguistically he is superior to me. He speaks his mother tongue, which unfortunately I am not yet so fluent in that I can effectively contradict him. This is what annoys me the most. Luckily, Trevor appears just in time. The colleague continues to provoke me but doesn't like that Trevor supports me. At some point, he withdraws. However, I am aware that from now on, he will not miss any opportunity to provoke me again and this turns out to be correct.

A few days later, there is another confrontation. The colleague reappears and starts provoking again. I try to keep calm, and not to react aggressively. However, it is difficult, and I get really angry inside. He doesn't stop and keeps annoying me. There's not much left before I smack him, which is exactly what he wants to achieve. He's far too weak for a fight and wants to provoke a punch from my side. If I did him this favour, I would be dismissed immediately. He's superior to me linguistically, which he is aware of, and continues to insult me. I become aggressive. He notices this and continues. Luckily, Trevor shows up in time again, otherwise, there might have been a real fight. Now Trevor takes on the provocateur, and his English is perfect. My rival didn't expect this and backed off. But he will take every opportunity to provoke me further. Luckily, today is Friday and I have the weekend to think about how I should behave in the future to avoid a conflict. I have to be careful, and must not allow myself to be provoked.

The carefree days are over. The nasty colleague never misses an opportunity to make my life difficult. Luckily, I can go to college every Friday night.

Autumn is passing, and December is coming. Time to contact some local schools and colleges to explore employment opportunities. This is harder than expected. I start looking in Derby. A week later I extended the application radius to Nottingham. However, without any success. One negative answer follows the other. My mood drops. I would like to change jobs and finally want to find qualified employment. The thought of qualifying myself for a sophisticated job through the training course has recently motivated me. However, with every refusal, hope dwindles together with motivation. The threshold of giving up is getting closer and closer. But, this line must never be reached! Giving up after everything that has already been achieved is out of the question. After all, we currently have two jobs.

It's now mid-December and I still couldn't find any employment opportunities at local schools or colleges. Finally, my persistence is rewarded. A college in Derby invites me for an interview with their German teacher. Finally, at least a small success.

The next evening after work I visited this college, met the teacher, and discussed a job opportunity. I learned that from January three A-level classes require supervision for learning German conversation skills. This doesn't sound bad. However, there is a disadvantage. Unfortunately, that would only be one hour per week per class, so together it only makes three hours a week. Currently, that is all she could offer me. However, the hour is well paid at £12. So I could earn £36 gross in three hours, basically the same amount as I earned in Belper for a whole week's manual labour.

I have to make a decision. I will earn less than at my current job but may be able to find more classes at other colleges. It would be a start. I thus decided to accept the post at the college and resigned from my job at the textile company just before Christmas to take on my new challenge on Monday, January 6th. The training course also ends in December and I receive my "Stage One Certificate", which I hope will open more doors for me at other schools or colleges in the future.

Christmas 1985. Since it is too expensive to visit both families, we decided to spend Christmas separately this year. Marie will travel to France to see her family, and I shall visit mine in Germany. She will go by coach, I will travel by train. Originally, I also wanted to go by coach, but I waited too long to buy the ticket and no seats were left.

On Saturday, December 21st, we take the bus from Duffield to Derby. From there, the journey continues to London by coach. We arrive in the capital at around 1 p.m. and have a few hours to stroll through the city. Marie's coach will leave at 7 p.m., while my train departs at 9 p.m.

At Victoria Bus Station there is a lot of activity. Long-distance coaches start from here to all parts of Europe. There are travellers everywhere with a lot of luggage. Everyone wants to go home for Christmas. After Marie's coach has left, I walk the short distance to Victoria Train Station.

When my train arrives at Dover, we are not allowed to board the ferry immediately, because the sea is too rough. After more than an hour, we can finally go on board. During the crossing, I try to sleep on a bench. From Ostend in Belgium, I take a train to Cologne. Unfortunately, we arrived there late, which meant that I had to wait for the next train to Frankfurt.

On Sunday, December 22nd, at around 5 p.m., I finally reached my destination and spent the Christmas holidays with my family. There is a lot to tell. Everyone is very curious and wants to know how we are doing.

FOURTH JOB
AS AN ASSISTANT
FOR GERMAN CONVERSATION
AT DERBY COLLEGE

On Monday, January 6, 1986, I started my new job at Derby College as an assistant for German conversation. I'm a bit nervous because I've never worked as a teacher before. For the first time, I am sitting in a staff room and preparing myself for the lesson.

At 9 a.m., the lesson starts. The first group consists of six students. According to the German teacher, the best students are in this group. It should thus be relatively easy to get them to talk, as they are very interested. The students should speak as much German as possible, that's the main task. The topics to be dealt with include forest decline in Germany, the carnival on the Rhine, and a discussion of the book "Die verlorene Ehre der Katharina Blum" (The Lost Honour of Katharina Blum) by Heinrich Böll.

The first lesson goes well, and the assistant and the students get to know each other. Some of the students speak German very well, and I am pleasantly surprised.

The next day, I teach the second group, have Wednesday off, and look after the third group on Thursday morning. With these two groups, I was warned that the conversation would be a little more difficult because the students don't speak German very well and are a bit shy. This information was accurate and the students usually only responded to my questions with "yes", "no", or "don't know". Therefore, it is important to find topics that interest them. What could teenagers be interested in? Holiday adventures, pets, hobbies? However, these topics don't really work either. Let's try movies, actors, music, and pop stars. That's better. The students become more relaxed and occasionally even utter complete sentences. While it is not easy to keep coming up with new questions for over an hour, they at least manage to converse with one another, and that's the main task.

I practically only work three hours a week, which gives me plenty of time to look for additional employment. During the third week of January, I visit various colleges in Mansfield, Nottingham and a private school on the Derbyshire/Staffordshire border. However, unfortunately without success. Although some of the colleges would be interested in an assistant for German, they lack the financial means to hire one. Such a position would have to be approved and that could take time. However, I cannot wait that long as I need more lessons now, and not in a year.

Hence, at the end of the week, I am still limited to only three lessons at Derby College. If I cannot get more, I'll have to come up with something else. I carefully consider my options and decide to visit large companies in Derby and Nottingham to possibly find a qualified job. My weekly income is currently £36 and Marie has a job at the building society. Hence, this time around, I do not have to accept any kind of work, and I could even be selective. Maybe I'll really manage to find a qualified job. During the following weeks, I put this into practice and started searching again.

Monday, January 13th. After the end of the lesson, I drive to Nottingham and visit the headquarters of the textile group of companies, in whose two subsidiaries I've already worked. If there are any business connections to Germany, I might be the right person. I managed to get through to the personnel office and was granted an interview, but nothing was decided today. In due course, I will be notified.

The next stop is a company that manufactures bicycles. At the reception, I am instructed to go to the HR department. There, I found out that unfortunately there are no vacancies at the moment, but that I should try the company just around the corner. From time to time, employees with foreign language skills are needed there.

The company in question manufactures car accessories and exports part of the production. Here I can also get through to the personnel office. Unfortunately, there are no vacancies in this company either. However, they show a general interest in an application and want to keep my documents. Should a job opportunity arise during the next few weeks, I will be notified immediately.

It is already after 3 p.m. and I've had enough for today. Any more negative experiences would only frustrate me now, so I stop and go home. Tomorrow is another day.

Tuesday, January 14th. Right after the lesson, I try my luck in Derby.

First I visit the manufacturer of locomotives and wagons. However, jobs are scarce there as well. Afterwards, I again try Rolls-Royce's aircraft engine division, but without success. It just won't work.

Wednesday, January 15th. I am not giving any lessons today and can thus already start my job search in the morning. I drive to the industrial estate east of Derby City Centre.

At a printing house, I can't get past the porter.

Next, I try at Rolls-Royce's nuclear division, but cannot get past the porter here either. However, the man is friendly and helpful and calls the HR department. Someone will come by to see me. I started gathering some hope, and saw myself in the HR office of this world-famous company and already employed in my wildest imagination. However, disillusionment promptly follows! An employee appears and hands me an application form to fill in. My application will then be checked. Unfortunately, more is not possible at the moment.

It is already afternoon. I want to make one more attempt today and drive to the headquarters of a large textile company on the outskirts of Derby. However, I have no luck there either, feel the frustration rising, break off, return home and fill in the Rolls-Royce application form. This is at least a small glimmer of hope on the otherwise unsuccessful horizon of today's job search.

Thursday, January 16th. This afternoon, I continued my job search.

The first address is a large wine merchant because anyone who imports German and French wines might need employees with relevant language skills. While this is a logical thought, unfortunately, this is not the case.

The next destination is a famous manufacturer of bone china in Derby whose products are well-known throughout the country. There, I received another application form but could not get any further either. However, it was worth trying.

The search continues. I head toward a large company that I've already noticed for a while. It is supposed to have business connections with Germany. So, let's give it a try. However, my approach abruptly ends here at the gate as well. The porter won't let me through and calls HR with the result that I should apply in writing.

There is only one area left that I would like to visit, namely the East Midlands airport, which is the joint airport of Derby, Nottingham and Leicester. However, it is too late for today and I'll try the airport tomorrow.

Friday, January 17th. I make my way to the airport early in the morning. Once there, I head straight for the administration building, where the offices of air freight companies are located, and walk down the corridor knocking on every door and asking for a job. I talk to a woman who just crosses my path, have to wait for a moment and can then talk to an HR person. Unfortunately, he cannot offer me anything suitable but if I'm interested, I should come back in early summer, then there could be jobs. During the summer months, temporary workers are always needed to load and unload the aircraft. Unfortunately, there is currently no need for this.

I keep on searching. Diagonally opposite the airport administration building, I notice a hangar where aeroplanes are repaired. The entrance is at the back of the building. The woman at reception calls HR and after a few minutes, an employee appears. I learned that they are looking for technicians and engineers. Unfortunately, I cannot offer these skills, but foreign languages. However, languages are not required here.

There is another company located directly opposite the hangar. I'm about to set off when I notice the name of the company. It looks familiar. I think for a moment, and then I remember. Of course, that's one of the companies I wrote to shortly after my arrival last year and received a negative reply. Nine months ago, employees with foreign language skills were not required there. I hesitate for a second. Does it really make sense to approach this company again if I've already received a written rejection?

I almost turn around, not wanting to try again, but change my mind at the last minute. Now that I am here, I definitely shouldn't miss an opportunity. Even if it won't bear fruit – and I am convinced that it will not – I won't have to blame myself later for not having really tried everything.

I reach the reception through the main entrance. The receptionist is on the phone. I wait until she's finished, get straight to the point, and ask for a job. Either there is work or there isn't. The woman behind the reception desk looks at me in astonishment, probably taking me for a sales representative. She seems to assume that I want to sell something. No, I don't want to sell anything, except for my labour if necessary. "I have foreign language skills to offer, do you need something like that?" "One moment please," she says, picking up the phone. A little later, a woman from the marketing department appears. I also briefly explained my request to her. She seems surprised too, and it is evident that she is trying to evaluate me. It is not every day that a German shows up out of nowhere on the doorstep of a company in the UK and asks for a job. She asks me to take a seat, and disappears, taking my CV with her. After a while, she returns accompanied by two men in dark suits and introduces them to me as the sales director and sales manager. The two invite me into an office room.

We take a seat at a conference table. I am asked to tell them something about my life, what I've done for a living, how long I've been in the country, why I came to the UK and so on. As I speak, they glance at my CV from time to time. They want to know whether I have any technical knowledge, and understand technical drawings to which I respond with a diplomatic "It depends." A technical drawing is spread out in front of me. Thanks to the school subject "engineering drawing", I have some idea of what it means and answer their questions about the drawing as best as I can. The answers don't seem too bad as the two are satisfied. They proceeded to tell me more about the company's products. They manufacture 3D coordinate measuring machines. The sales manager studies my CV again and picks up the phone. Shortly thereafter, another employee appears, who is introduced to me as the application engineer. He also reads through my CV with interest. At the end, he nods a few times in approval.

I've been here for over an hour now. Everything happened so quickly, that I still can't really believe it. I am starting to realize that this is a professional interview and I am determined to seize the opportunity. If there is a job, I shall fight to get it.

It's noon and I'm invited to lunch. Not a bad sign. If they even entertain me, my chances are certainly not too bad. We drive to a local pub. I have little appetite as I am much too excited and just have a sandwich. Both of my interlocutors decide to have a full pub meal. The portions look very appetising, but I couldn't eat this right now. I am very nervous about the outcome of this conversation. Could there really be a job for me at this company?

After an hour, we return to the office. They inform me in more detail about the company. It has existed for twenty-five years and has been part of an American group of companies for one year. This sounds interesting. Once they are done, I am led into a work-shop where some of the measuring machines are located. A young engineer is programming one of them, and he shows me around and explains how it works. As far as the technology is concerned, I'm a bit lost at the moment. After about half an hour, it's back to the sales manager's office. Another application engineer joins the discussion.

We are slowly approaching the moment I've been waiting for. Do they have an open position here or not? They have one! At least that's what the sales manager says. One of their employees speaks Italian, and another speaks French but nobody in the company speaks German. Since the company also maintains business connections with Germany and intends to expand these further in the coming years, they have been looking for someone who speaks German for quite some time. All this is beginning to seem like a wonderful dream from which I could suddenly wake up. Somehow everything is too good to be true. However, it is not a dream, it's actually reality. The sales manager notes that they intended to invite an applicant from a German-speaking country for an interview. But since I'm already here, live nearby, and my education plus foreign language skills would fit, I could actually be offered the job, provided I was interested.

First of all, I am completely speechless! I would never have expected such an offer this morning, and would not have dared to even remotely dream of it. I am currently being offered a qualified job that requires German language skills. As the job interests me, I take it immediately. I definitely will not let such an opportunity go by. The sales manager suggests beginning with a temporary job contract for three months starting on Monday. I should translate German and English texts to prove myself. During these three months, my gross income would be £100 a week. I accept the offer.

Just after 3 p.m., I leave this company as a winner. I found a very promising new job. Who knows what else could become of it? Although it is initially limited to three months, the employment can be extended if I meet the requirements and now it is up to me to fulfil them.

Suddenly, I think of my job at the college. Now that I've found a full-time job, I cannot continue teaching for three mornings per week. It would thus be best to stop by immediately and inform the German teacher about my new situation. Naturally, she is disappointed to lose her language assistant after just one week but she understands my position and the fact that I cannot turn down a job offer like this because of three hours a week at the college. Since I do not have a permanent employment contract, it is not a problem for me to leave at short notice.

However, to support the students, I offer to hold evening conversation lessons in a pub in Duffield on Sunday evenings. Anyone interested could communicate with me there in German. Many are interested and almost all students show up on the first Sunday. Unfortunately, it is far too loud in a pub to be able to have a decent conversation and thus, in the second week, fewer students appear, and in the third week there are only a few left. It was worth the try. My time as a language assistant for German at Derby College was thus very brief - I couldn't have known that I would be able to find a qualified full-time job so quickly.

After the college was informed, I returned home. This success should now be duly celebrated. However, at first, I don't say anything when I arrive home and instead suggest that we go to the local pub for a glass of wine. Marie agrees. As we sit comfortably in the pub, I put the cards on the table. What a wonderful feeling to be successful! We enjoy it and are both very happy.

FIFTH JOB
AS A TEMPORARY ASSISTANT
FOR TRANSLATIONS

Sunday, January 19th. In the evening I go for a walk, as I want to be alone and think. Tomorrow is my first workday at the new company. How will I be accepted there? What will my tasks be? These are all questions on the eve of taking up a new job.

How many times have I started something new? I count and it's seven times during the last five years. I have had to get used to new working groups and products quite often during the past few years, which I've always managed well.

It is already dark and I walk in the dim light of the street lamps. The walk does me good. I'm ready to start tomorrow with commitment and intend to make the most of this great opportunity.

Every new professional start is difficult. On my first day, I felt a bit lost, and my new colleagues were reserved towards me. I am placed at a conference table in the middle of an open-plan office, as another workspace is currently not available. I translate some texts, study information brochures about the company's products, am "the new bloke", and feel it. Nobody speaks to me directly or asks anything. From time to time, my colleagues glance at me from a distance and certainly talk about me. But, everything takes time and this situation will surely change in a few days.

My new workplace is located at the East Midlands airport, south of Derby. The office building is on the northern side of the airport terminal, and the production facility is on the southern side. The company employs around one hundred members of staff in total.

During the first few days, I will provisionally be sitting at the round conference table. However, I am promised that this will soon change.

I gradually get used to the work and am tasked with translating texts and calling suppliers in Germany. I also get to know my new colleagues better. During the breaks, I join them, and they show interest in me and ask questions. I am told that before I joined this company, all German texts had to be sent to a translation agency in Nottingham, which not only took time but was also expensive. Since I joined the company, this process has greatly improved. My boss is happy about this, and so am I. It's definitely more pleasant working in an office than in a warehouse. Unfortunately, there is no canteen and at lunchtime, someone comes around and sells sandwiches, cakes, and fruit. A few colleagues go to the nearby pub to enjoy a warm meal.

As for Marie's current job, we made the right decision regarding the choice between the chocolate factory and the building society. At the end of her temporary employment, a position in another department is advertised internally. Marie applies for it, is already known within the company, and her current boss speaks up for her. She gets the job. This time, it is a full-time position, and she's even being taken on as a permanent employee. Her gross income is £90 a week. Compared to her, I do not yet have a permanent employment contract, as my job is currently still restricted.

In February, Marie's sister comes to visit us for two weeks. She is the second family visitor after my brother.

One morning in March, my boss called me to tell me that he was satisfied with the quality of my work and would therefore extend my employment until the end of September. I would also get a pay rise and would now earn £120 gross a week.

When one considers that just eight months ago I was only making £45 a week, my income has almost tripled in this time. The risk of changing jobs has paid off. After one year in the UK, we are both successful. Marie has a permanent employment contract with a building society, I have a fixed-term contract, but a solid position with a mechanical engineering company. Together, we now have a gross income of £210 a week, which is £840 per month. We have settled in, made friends, moved into a nice flat, and are very pleased.

Our second springtime in Britain. Actually, it is only my second springtime, since Marie didn't move to the UK until July last year. Many of our English friends say that springtime is the loveliest season in the UK, and they are correct. A splendour of flowers unfolds in the gardens and parks everywhere that is second to none.

Above all, it's getting warmer which is very pleasant after the cold winter months. Although our flat is very comfortable in the warm season, it can get very frosty in winter. But, the cold months are over now, so why bother worrying about it?

Currently, I still drive the car we brought along from Germany, which has its steering wheel on the left. It is a strange feeling as a driver sitting on the left side of the vehicle and having to drive on the left side of the road at the same time - fortunately, it has been going well for almost nine months and I haven't caused an accident (yet). However, due to the vehicle's set-up, one always has to drive with extreme concentration and can never rely on one's routine way of driving, as otherwise, one could end up on the wrong side of the road.

Everything went well until the beginning of February. I'm driving down a lane, correctly on the left, looking for a parking space. I spot one to the right, think I've found the entrance, and turn off. The supposed entrance soon turns out to be a footpath. I reverse and let the car slowly roll straight ahead looking for the entrance. Suddenly, some distance ahead, I notice a stationary vehicle on my side of the road. This is still nothing unusual, because now and then cars stop briefly in the opposite direction to let someone out. Suddenly, I realize that I am on the wrong side of the road, not the vehicle in front of me and I immediately return to the left side.

This incident greatly concerned me. Luckily nothing happened, but it could have been worse as I drove on the right side of the lane for a while without realising it. That evening, for the first time, I thought about selling the car and getting a vehicle with the steering wheel on the right-hand side. But who in the UK wants to buy a car with the driver's seat on the left? Time will tell.

I look at adverts for second-hand cars, intend to invest around £400, and would like to get a VW Beetle and thus concentrate particularly on this type of vehicle. There are some on offer, but they are either too expensive or not in good condition.

I turn my attention to other makes and come across a Renault 5. The advert is promising, and the price is within my budget. In the evening, I call the garage and look at the car. Its body is fine. I take a test drive, during which I have to get used to changing gears with the left hand, even though my right hand automatically twitches and misses the gear stick. The engine runs quietly and, all in all, I'm quite pleased. What can you expect for £400? The garage would even trade my current car for £100. It is certainly not worth more because it's old, starting to rust, and the steering wheel is on the wrong side. Hence, I'm quite happy to get rid of it.

However, it's not that simple as the vehicle is still subject to special customs regulations. Therefore, I am not allowed to sell it within one year after importation. If I do, a tax will be due. Unfortunately, the year is not quite over yet and I thus need to find out what the tax amount will be.

The next day, I called the customs office in Derby and was told to bring the car in for an appraisal. I see them during the lunch break. The vehicle is valued at £2,000. This amount seems way too high! The MOT has almost expired and the steering wheel is on the wrong side. Nobody pays £2,000 for such a car. However, the tax value depends on the year of manufacture. Should I sell the car before the end of the year, a tax of £300 would be levied. After that, I can freely sell the vehicle. It's March now. Therefore, the car is still subject to special customs regulations and thus I still have to keep it for a while.

I pay £400 for the Renault and park the old car under the chestnut tree behind the house where it stays for three months as no one wants it. At the beginning of summer, a neighbour mentioned that the space behind the house was a car park and not a scrapyard. The hint is clear, the old car has to go. With a bit of luck, I sold it to a garage for spare parts for £30. In the end, they must have found a buyer, because a few weeks later we noticed the car on the road again. The fact that the steering wheel is on the wrong side didn't deter the new owner, while for my part I'm happy to have a car with the driver's seat on the right side.

During the weekend, we take some friends out into the country-side in our new car. The first part of the journey runs smoothly, and the second-hand car drives properly. Around noon, we stop and have a picnic. However, when I try to start the engine after the break, nothing happens. The battery is empty. One of our friends found the cause pretty quickly: the generator is defective, and it no longer charges the battery. We push the car, the engine starts, and fortunately, we can drive on. However, our planned dinner has to be cancelled as we have to be home before dark because the headlights won't work without a charged battery.

The car has to go back to the garage the following Monday. Luckily, they respond courteously and fit a replacement generator free of charge. After that incident, the car no longer causes any problems. On the whole, it was a good buy for £400.

In April, we visit our Australian friends Debby and Andrew in Cambridge. It is our first visit to this world-famous university town and we immediately fall in love with its special flair. Our friends live right in the centre of town. On our first evening in Cambridge, we attend a theatre performance at a college. Students perform the play "The Visit of the Old Lady" by Friedrich Dürrenmatt. On Sunday, we stroll through the streets and in the evening we go to the cinema and, to Marie's delight, we watch a film in French. At the end of this visit, we decided to return for punting in the summer and are already looking forward to it.

Another family visit is scheduled for the end of May. This time, my parents are coming over for a week and I fetch them from Birmingham airport. During the following week, we show them as much of the Derbyshire countryside as possible. Friends also invited us for dinner, so that my parents also get to know an English family. Unfortunately, the week passes far too quickly.

At work, I familiarise myself with all the requirements of the job, translate texts, write telexes, call suppliers in German-speaking countries, relieve colleagues of administrative work, and receive my own telephone set.

At the moment, I'm more satisfied with my work than ever before. Even on Sunday evenings, I look forward to going back to work the next day.

At present, I have to type translations into the system using a colleague's computer monitor as I unfortunately do not have my own monitor yet. One day, there are two older devices on the floor in the aisle. New equipment has been installed at two workplaces. What happens to these two devices? A monitor of my own would make work easier. I approach my boss. He also likes the idea and promises to take care of it. Indeed, one of these devices was already available to me the next morning. From this day on, work is even more fun. I now have my own desk with a telephone set and monitor, and my workplace is becoming increasingly professional.

A very special job is waiting for me at the beginning of June. An informative meeting between German engineers and representatives of British companies will take place in London on Friday, June 13th. The sponsor of this meeting is an MP (member of parliament) on behalf of the British Overseas Trade Board and the Machine Tool Trades Association. My boss intends to take part and I am asked to accompany him to translate if necessary. That's the plan.

Shortly before leaving, my boss explained that he had to keep another appointment and therefore could not come with me. I should travel to London on my own and represent him.

While I was quite surprised at first, I soon considered this challenge as a unique opportunity to distinguish myself, and thus take the train to London and meet my fellow countrymen. A little small talk here, a chat over a glass of wine there, while I try to represent "my British company" as well as I can. The exchange of ideas in a relaxed atmosphere is followed by a tour through the Houses of Parliament including a dinner at the Palace of Westminster. In the House of Commons, I can also stand for a moment at the spot where the Prime Minister gives his speeches. This is a very special highlight! After the tour, we are escorted to a dining room within the Houses of Parliament, where an unforgettable dinner awaits us. You don't experience something like this every day.

With little luggage but a lot of courage, I landed on the coast of this country a little over a year ago. Now I dine with British and German engineers and businessmen at the heart of this country's power. What an achievement!

Shortly thereafter, my boss wants to find out how I can deal with customers as, so far, I have mainly worked in the office. The latest machine tools are to be demonstrated to domestic customers at an in-house exhibition. I was assigned to a pre-setting tool from a Swiss manufacturer, and two Swiss engineers would come to demonstrate the tool. I should only translate if necessary, which shouldn't be too difficult.

However, things turn out very differently as the two engineers are unable to attend for some reason. This important message is only communicated to me shortly before the start of the exhibition. I am informed that I have to demonstrate the pre-setting tool all by myself because my colleagues are all assigned to other tasks. What on earth am I supposed to do now? I'm not a technical engineer and therefore don't know much about technology. Now good advice is essential, and I quickly receive some basic information about how the tool works.

The exhibition starts the next day. I had hoped until the last minute that the Swiss engineers would turn up after all. However, since this is not the case, I have to face up to this challenge. I will do my very best, although I'm not quite sure how.

So, here I am, a German, standing in front of a Swiss machine tool in Great Britain and am supposed to demonstrate a pre-setting tool that I know nearly nothing about to a local specialist audience. Great prospects!

The first group appears. I was told that every group would remain at each machine for ten minutes. Do I have enough technical knowledge to be able to talk for ten minutes about the tool assigned to me? At first, I roughly explain its functions. Two minutes have passed, and eight minutes are left. I now start to talk about more complicated issues and promptly run into trouble. I can manage three more minutes, then I run out of knowledge. There are five minutes left. So, what to do? I know that in each group there are always a few specialists who would like to share their technical knowledge with others. If you ask these people for an explanation, they feel honoured. Their expertise is recognised, they are asked for advice, willingly provide information, and explain everything you want to hear. It is the same with my first group. When I run out of knowledge, I use this insight, ask the visitors to take a closer look at the tool, take this opportunity to ask questions myself, have the technique explained to me in detail and thus receive more information for the next group. This tactic works. The engineers remain in front of the tool for five minutes, discussing and explaining.

After this, the groups rotate and new engineers gather around my machine, whose functionality I know a bit better now. I'm able to explain technical details for about five minutes, risking another two minutes on "slippery ice", and then have them step forward again, inspect the tool, and ask more questions myself. In this way, I learn more and more about the pre-setting tool.

A total of twelve groups are guided from machine to machine.

When the fifth group approaches, I've acquired enough technical knowledge to cover the entire ten minutes and with each new group, I become more confident.

On the second day of the exhibition, I explained the tool to another twelve groups of visitors and also met the owner of the German company with whom we work very closely. The family business is based near Frankfurt and also manufactures measuring machines that we sell in Britain and some other countries. We also purchase material for our machines from this company.

At the beginning of summer, we attend a family reunion in France. This time we take the plane to avoid the long journey by bus or train. The flight from the East Midlands airport to Paris takes just under one hour. We entrust our lives to a medium-sized Fokker Friendship propeller plane. The flight is smooth, and our "bird" doesn't vibrate too much. We reach the south coast of England and have a marvellous view of the English Channel. After landing in Paris, we take a train further south.

The reunion takes place on a farm in glorious summer weather. There are fine meats from the barbecue, various salads, and red wine, and we dance until late at night. There is a lot to tell. Everyone wants to know how we are doing on the other side of the English Channel. Altogether, we stay in France for a week.

The return flight is smooth at the beginning until we approach for landing. Due to strong gusts of wind, the small propeller plane is shaken up extremely hard for a few minutes. Sometimes it tilts to the left, then to the right, and suddenly it drops down so that the seat literally breaks away from under your bottom. This is not very pleasant! Many passengers are worried and I have to admit that I don't feel particularly well either. Hope we'll be down soon. We continue to be shaken for a few minutes before we finally have solid ground under our feet again.

We spend July in Derbyshire, drive to the nearby mountains on the weekends, and visit the sights of this beautiful area, particularly Matlock Bath. This place is well known and therefore very busy, especially during the summer months. We stroll along the main street, past tearooms, fish and chip shops, souvenir shops, and amusement arcades, drink our afternoon tea, and eat tasty sandwiches and delicious cakes. These are wonderful carefree summer days, we are happy and content and can enjoy ourselves with no troubles or concerns.

A two-week holiday in August is ideal for a bike tour through Cornwall and we set out on Saturday, August 24th. Equipped with a tent, sleeping bags, air mattresses, and other vital baggage we cycle to Derby train station. From there, an Intercity train takes us to Exeter in Devon. Reservations for bicycles are required for this express train. From Exeter, we then take a passenger train to Penzance which is situated on the western tip of Cornwall.

We arrive there during the late afternoon and first head towards the campsite. There are only a few tents, we are almost alone and can choose a site. After our tent has been pitched and the luggage stowed away, we head for the beach where we discover "St. Michael's Mount", the little brother of the more familiar "Le Mont-Saint-Michel" across the Channel in France.

Our first night in the tent does not start very pleasantly because of a pub right next door. Around 1 a.m., the last quite drunken guests leave the pub, and some of them stagger across the campsite. We lie in our sleeping bags and hope not to be bothered. Some of the revellers try to open people's tents and we hear the voices of angry campers who don't like this at all. Our tent is a bit offside and we hope that we don't get any trouble now. We do not have a vehicle to retrieve, just our bikes behind the tent. Here we are in our sleeping bags and hope that the drunken revellers will soon find their way home. Luckily, it stays calm around our tent, and the voices become quieter, and slowly move away towards the locality. Soon, peace is restored and we relax and try to sleep, although we don't quite succeed during this first night of camping.

Rain in the morning, what a great start! We wait for the rain to stop, dismantle the tent, stow the luggage on our bicycles, and set off towards Land's End, the most southwestern point of mainland Great Britain.

We stop at a tearoom for breakfast. Marie chooses a continental breakfast, while I prefer a tasty English breakfast with sausages, bacon, scrambled eggs, baked mushrooms, baked tomatoes, and black pudding.

At Land's End, we take a photo like all other tourists. In front of us lies the vast Atlantic Ocean - a terrific expanse of water that separates us from America. Due to the many tourists, we don't stay here long, but get back on our bicycles and find tranquillity in a small village whose local pub invites us for lunch. We both chose lamb, and it tastes great!

During the late afternoon, we discover a campsite next to the narrow coastal road. The sanitary facilities are sparkling clean, and we love it. After pitching our tent, we walk along the rocky cliffs. Many tin mines used to be active here, and we encounter history at every turn. What a stunning landscape! Rocky cliffs, a rough sea, and ruins of former mines between the rocks. We sit on a cliff high above the sea and look out at the ocean. It is quiet, and only in the distance, the sound of a ship's horn breaks through the foggy solitude. Around us, there is only peace and tranquillity.

On our second night, we sleep much better and nothing disturbs us. In the morning, even though it's raining heavily we have to move on, and we dismantle the tent and load the bikes. Since we haven't had breakfast yet, our stomachs are growling. We are soon completely soaked, and our mood deteriorates. No breakfast, plenty of water from above, something has to change. Luckily, we spot a tearoom in the next village. Let's go in. A wonderful breakfast with tea, scones, jam and clotted cream awaits us in a cosy dining room. It tastes delicious! Outside, the rain is pouring, but this no longer bothers us. After this perfect breakfast, we are so content that this horrible weather no longer affects us at all. No matter how awful it is, we cycle towards St. Ives in a good mood.

After our arrival there, we have some problems finding the campsite. Finally, we get there, pitch the tent, and explore our surroundings. We like St. Ives. With its narrow streets and quaint shops, this place exudes southern flair and it is hard to believe that we are still in England.

In the late afternoon, the weather changes - all of a sudden, the grey clouds disappear and reveal a bright blue sky - and after the heavy rainfall this morning, it's almost unreal.

We spend the next day at the beach. It is hot, the complete opposite of yesterday's weather. However, the seawater is very cold and I can't stay in it for long. Due to the constant wind, I underestimate the intensity of the sunlight and the result is a perfect sunburn in the evening.

The next day, we take the train to St. Austell as we've agreed to meet Debby and Andrew, our friends from Cambridge, there on the following day as we want to cycle to Plymouth together. The brilliant weather continues, and we can pitch our tent in bright sunshine at the St. Austell campsite.

In the afternoon we visit Mevagissey. Unlike St. Ives, there are no crowds of tourists here. We drink tea, eat scones, and sun-bathe on the harbour wall. Hopefully, the brilliant weather will last until we reach Plymouth. Unfortunately, that only remains a wish, as the British Isles always have a surprise in store as far as the weather is concerned.

The next morning it rains heavily and we cannot believe our eyes. Everything could have been so nice. Our mood drops and hits an all-time low in the afternoon. Completely soaked, we almost want to abandon our plans and take the next train home. However, that's not possible as our friends will arrive tonight as agreed. Fortunately, it stops raining in the evening and we cycle to St. Austell train station.

Debby and Andrew arrive on time, and it's already dark. After they have pitched their tent, we slip into our sleeping bags and rest to be fit for tomorrow. We have ambitious plans for the next few days and hope for better weather.

In the morning, the sun does not shine, but at least there is no more rain. However, after we've dismantled the tents, it starts to drizzle. Even though it doesn't rain heavily all day, somehow everything is wet. We cycle along the coast, and while the landscape is stunning, the weather isn't. We want to spend the night in the dry and proceed to look for a hostel. After finding suitable accommodation, we spend the night in a warm, dry bed which greatly improves our mood.

The next day, it stopped raining and now cycling along the south coast of England is really fun. Around noon, the sun even appears and the sky becomes clear.

This evening, we camp again, as the weather is fine. I visit the local pub together with Andrew to try a "dangerous drink", an extra strong cider that is said to only exist here in Cornwall. According to Andrew, it is so potent that just "A pint of that beverage and you're drunk." I don't know this particularly strong cider, at least not yet, and so I'm quite keen to try its effects. However, we're out of luck, as this pub doesn't offer it any more. While it has been served in the past, too many guests became drunk too quickly and thus they decided not to sell it any longer. We try another pub but have no luck there either. It must have been extreme, this extra strong cider! So we have a few pints of beer instead and the secret of the "Cornwall cider" will probably elude me forever, whereby maybe it is better that way.

Our wives, meanwhile, preferred to stay at the campsite. When we return from our pub tour, we want to scare them a bit and act like we are both very drunk, telling them that we each drank two pints of this extremely strong cider. Apparently, we acted very convincingly because at first, they believed us before we admitted that we only had a few pints of beer and were still almost sober.

A pleasant day, including a nice evening, comes to an end.

Today is the last day of our cycling tour through Cornwall. In the afternoon, we reach Plymouth, take a small ferry from Cornwall to Devon, and look for the youth hostel. The hostel warden is quite surprised when he learns the nationalities of our small travel group. Two Australians, a Frenchwoman, and a German, travelling together in the south of England. You certainly don't encounter that every day, even in a youth hostel.

Our last night is very noisy. Andrew and I have to stay in a large dormitory with thirty beds. In the evening, all beds are occupied, and the great snoring contest begins. When one stops, another snorer starts somewhere else. While I don't get much sleep that night, I at least can catch up on some sleep during the train back to Derby the next day. From Derby train station, we cycle the last few kilometres to our flat.

An interesting week in Cornwall comes to an end and, apart from the two rainy days, we really enjoyed it.

September 1986. Shortly after our vacation, I have to go to Germany on business as the German company we work with is organizing an in-house exhibition. This is a new challenge and I fly from Birmingham to Frankfurt/Main together with an application engineer. During the in-house exhibition, I acted as a translator for the technical engineer but also soon started explaining our measuring machine to visitors on my own. Thus, I get to know and understand the technology even more intensively and can combine theory and practice. My boss is also present and I know he's watching me to observe my interactions with customers and how well I understand the technology. Since I am aware that a lot depends on my performance at this event as my current employment contract only runs until the end of this month, I do my best and am quite satisfied with my performance. I'm sure I'll soon find out whether my boss sees it the same way.

Saturday, September 13th. I fly back to Birmingham from Frankfurt in the evening. We start in a light drizzle, submerge into dense fog, and visibility is limited. Then comes what is probably the most beautiful moment of a flight. The wall of fog parts and gives way to a bright blue sky. In the west, the sun is already turning slightly reddish - what a heavenly moment! We glide into another world. The last shreds of clouds disperse, and our plane climbs higher into the clear evening sky. When we have reached our final cruising altitude, our "bird" glides calmly through the evening sunshine.

As I look out of the window, I think back to the past one and a half years that I've been in the UK. In March 1985 I would never have dared to dream that I could get a job abroad like the one I have at the moment. At that time, I was travelling across the sea on an overnight ferry, towards a completely uncertain future. I had courage and was determined to live and work in the UK for two years, come what may. Now I'm sitting in the business class of a jet, drinking wine, eating smoked salmon, travelling again from Germany to the UK, only with the difference that I know exactly what to expect. I have a comfortable flat, an interesting job, good friends, and feel at home in Derbyshire. The risky decision to go abroad has paid off. High above the clouds, I enjoy the sweet feeling of success to the fullest.

EMPLOYMENT CONTRACT AS "TECHNICAL SUPPORT ENGINEER"

Two weeks later, my boss called me into his office. Now it's getting serious. What did he decide? The decision is positive and he offered me a permanent employment contract although the salary has not yet been determined and still has to be discussed with management. What is certain, however, is that I will be given a permanent contract as of October 1st, 1986. Even if my future income is not yet fixed, I am assured that it will satisfy me.

In the evening, I discuss the offer with Marie. While it doesn't come as a surprise as I've been expecting it for some time, we now have to make a decision. According to the original plan, we were only going to stay in the UK for two years, and this period is almost up. If I accept the contract, we will have to extend our stay.

We come to a decision. If the contract is financially worthwhile, I will accept it. This would extend our stay in the UK by at least two more years. The job is interesting, and I'm well-integrated and accepted by my colleagues. For my later career, more than two years of experience in a foreign country is certainly more positive than negative. We also like Derbyshire, have many good friends, and would like to stay here for a few more years.

However, there is one condition. If we stay, then we'll look for a larger, especially winterproof flat. I already know that it will be difficult for us to leave the cosy flat in Duffield in which we have felt very comfortable for two years. The house is quite old and old English houses are said to be haunted. I don't really believe in ghosts. But if they exist, then there must be a very good spirit in this house. I have never felt so safe and secure in a flat as I do here in the heart of England. It will be difficult for us to leave.

I have to wait a little longer for the employment contract but am assured that I will definitely receive it. What interests me most is the salary. Perhaps this impatience is typically German because my English colleagues don't seem to understand it. I will get the contract, that's for sure. For them, it doesn't matter when. The higher salary would be paid retrospectively as of October 1st, so what's the problem? The British and Germans seem to think differently here.

Four more weeks pass and there is still no contract, which is starting to annoy me. I start to apply some pressure and talk to the sales manager. Although he seems to take my concerns seriously, I can tell from his facial expression that he also doesn't understand my impatience. He assures me that I am already employed permanently and will receive a higher salary from October 1st. I give up. To the British, a signed contract just doesn't seem to have the same importance as it does to a German. What counts here is the word, the promise that was given. It is incomprehensible to my colleagues why I don't want to rely on it.

Two more weeks pass, and still no contract. I trust and keep waiting. After a few more days, I finally received my first permanent employment contract in Britain. Now it's official and I'm pleased. My annual salary will be £10,000 plus a special bonus of £1,000 to be paid in March. All employees who are not directly involved in the monthly sales bonus receive this special bonus. Hence, my total annual income will be £11,000 which amounts to £212 per week. Compared to the £35 that I earned from my first job in the UK, I've been able to increase my income significantly. Marie currently earns around £5,000 a year and financially we are doing well now. After a year and a half in the UK, we break even and cash injections are no longer required from our savings accounts.

To properly celebrate the contract, we visit a small restaurant that we always go to for special occasions. Marie chooses a shrimp cocktail to start, followed by grilled chicken breast with a side salad and a pancake with vanilla ice cream for dessert. I decide on a soup as a starter, a beef burger with cottage cheese as a main course, and also choose the filled pancake for dessert. We drink freshly squeezed orange juice with it. It tastes delicious! What a great feeling to be completely satisfied with little. We enjoy the evening to the fullest and don't want to swap places with anyone.

It's the end of November and winter is rapidly approaching. We start preparing for the cold season and winterproof the sliding windows. From last winter, we know what lies ahead of us and prepare for it accordingly. The windows are sealed on the inside with plastic foil so that the frost cannot penetrate. As the nights get colder, we use our sleeping bags below the covers. This is how we got through last winter.

December, Christmas time. Christmas cards are sent to friends and family. These cards are set up or hung up in long rows. We had to get used to this tradition and also send cards. It is taken very seriously here and we don't want to risk any friendships because we can't handle the "Christmas card ritual". Hence, we draw up a list with the names of everyone we know, buy a lot of Christmas cards, sign them (the text is already pre-printed), and send them off. That's basically all you have to do. Naturally, we also receive many cards and hang them on a string across the living room, as we have seen our friends do. Christmas time in England.

This year, Marie and I want to spend Christmas together, not separately with our respective families in two different countries like last year.

On December 24th, we work until noon after which I visit a pub with colleagues. Around 3 p.m., the first ones set off for home and I'm also drawn home now. We bought a festively decorated Christmas tree for the living room. After dark, we eat Scottish smoked salmon with toast, butter and lemon slices, drink dry white wine, and enjoy a delicious apple strudel baked by a local Austrian. While it's the second time that we're not spending Christmas with at least one of our families, Christmas Eve 1986 is still something very special. After our dinner, we go into our large living room, light up some candles, sit under the tree, and open the presents that we've received from family and friends. The gas fire imparts a cosy warmth, and only the mighty chestnut tree is watching us from outside the flat.

On New Year's Eve, we are invited to Irene and John's. Debby and Andrew have arrived from Cambridge, together with Andrew's parents from Australia and two aunts, to celebrate with us. Irene surprises us with a wonderful buffet. One can think what one wants about English cuisine, it is better than its reputation. In Britain, as in all countries, it depends on where and with whom you dine. The buffet tonight is not only delicious but also lovingly prepared to delight the eye. There are various salads, small pizzas, sausages, cheeses, sandwiches, fruit, cakes, pastries, puddings and, as a highlight, Irene's homemade filled chocolates. They taste incredibly good and comprise a chocolate shell filled with a mousse of rum-soaked fruit, surrounded by a crown of fresh cream and garnished with a glacé cherry. Delicious!

Until the turn of the year, we pass the time with lively conversations. Then, it's midnight: 1986 is ending, and making way for

1987. What awaits us in the new year? Will we continue to be as successful as before? Or will the winning streak come to an abrupt end at some point? We shall see. Everyone hugs each other and exchanges good wishes for a healthy new year. People from England, France, Australia, and Germany wish each other all the best in the early hours of 1987. If this isn't an international New Year!

At 1 a.m., we go home. It's not far, just ten minutes by car.

The turn of the year always has something sad and exciting at the same time. Familiar things come to an end, and new challenges arise.

Since the decision to accept the employment contract and to stay in the UK longer than originally planned also means finding a larger residential property to rent, the time has come to realize this intention.

On Saturday, January 3rd, I started searching, whereby this is easier said than done. I visit just about every major estate agent in Derby. There is a lot on offer to buy, but unfortunately, not much to rent. I walk from one real estate agency to another, it's raining, and the weather is frustrating. I try not to lose my motivation. Somewhere, I will find what I am looking for, I just have to be patient.

I try my luck with smaller agencies, and things look a bit more positive there. From time to time, I'm told, there are rental properties. However, nothing is available at the moment.

I kept searching, visited almost all the agencies, and finally received an address. A real estate agent can offer me a small house for rent in a western suburb of Derby.

On Sunday, January 4th, we take a look at the house from the outside. Like most houses in this residential area, the rental property is a semi-detached house with a front garden, garage, and back garden. The rent would be £180 per month. We like the house and the area. But before we decide, we would like to see the interior. Above all, we are interested in central heating and winterproof windows. I call the agent to arrange a viewing. Unfortunately, that won't be possible before the end of the week. I make an appointment for Saturday morning. However, I should have decided more quickly, because on Saturday the house was already rented out to someone else who decided before we did. Bad luck!

Hence, this rental property is gone and we regret our hesitation. Maybe we should have acted faster. But perhaps it's better that way, because what would we gain from renting a house with leaky windows, where it's not much warmer during the cold season than in our current flat? We don't rent anything without precise information. That's what we've decided to do, and that's how we're going to do it. So, let's forget about this house. It's gone, and regret doesn't help at this stage.

How do we receive more addresses of rental properties? Almost all adverts are uninteresting. Either the rental property is too small, too expensive, or fully furnished, which is unsuitable for us because we have our own furniture.

One day, I discovered an agency that specializes in rentals and visited them. Right from the start, I learned that nothing is available at the moment, and before I can receive any information on vacant properties, I have to pay £35 and only then can I view a list of around one hundred addresses of rental properties in the Derby area. Before I pay, I make sure that the addresses also include offers from pleasant residential areas. I am assured that offers from all neighbourhoods are on the list. I pay and have to wait a few minutes. Then I receive a copy of the address list.

Unfortunately, many properties are already marked as "rented". After a closer look, I realize that around half of the one hundred addresses are already let. Hence the £35 covers only half of the promised number of addresses. This doesn't look very serious! I complain and am told that there are new offers every day and of course, I have the right to see them as well. All I can do now is to make the best of the situation and study all the offers that are still available and I thus carefully review the remaining fifty or so properties on today's list. My apprehension is confirmed. Many of the properties on offer are located in less pleasant residential areas.

However, I then discover a bungalow and a semi-detached house. I will call the landlords of these two properties tomorrow from the office. Maybe I'm lucky. However, there is no success. The bungalow is only rented on a fully furnished basis to old-age pensioners, the semi-detached house is far too expensive and is only supposed to be available for one year as the owner wants to move back in afterwards.

Every evening after work I stop by this agency, which luckily is on my way home, and view the latest version of the list of rental properties. Most of the time, the offers hardly change at all, often even in a negative sense, since even more offers are marked as "already let". However, I won't give up. I've paid, so I'm going to visit them until something suitable comes up.

From time to time, there are some interesting offers, like a house in a pleasant neighbourhood that came up one day. I called the landlord and arranged a viewing for Sunday afternoon. Unfortunately, this does not lead to success either. The house is very nice, we like it, but it is fully furnished and can only be let for six months. This time frame is too short as we want to rent something for at least two years.

Saturday, January 31st. We spend the morning in Nottingham, and our mood could be better. We've been looking for a new home for four weeks now. Unfortunately without success so far. How do we get interesting addresses of rental properties?

A colleague gave me the tip to try the Derby Information Centre as it also provides information on rental flats and houses. It's definitely worth a try.

We decided to stop by there today, return to Derby, find the centre and enter. The interior is very clean, quite the opposite of the "35-pound agency". While nothing is free of charge here either, the fee is much cheaper. For only £5, one can look at the object list in this Information Centre for one month, and the information is updated every week. We pay the (fair) price and receive a folder with offers for various rental properties which are very well described and clearly divided into different residential areas. We looked through the folder, found a few suitable offers, and noted the addresses of three houses that would fit both in terms of location and rent. However, we don't know their state yet.

Later that evening, I called the landlords. The first offer is a fully furnished holiday home in the countryside that is only to be let for a few months. The next offer is a detached house in Derby. However, this house can also only be let for a limited period, and it is only available for one year.

Now there is only one address left. It is a semi-detached house in the countryside not far from Duffield and is still available with an unlimited rental period. This would suit us and I arranged a viewing for the next day. The house is located in Blackbrook, a small hamlet just outside Belper where only a few houses are lined up along the main road and a side street. The houses are surrounded by a rural idyll with green meadows, scattered trees, hedges, and pastures. The rental property is currently occupied by an elderly couple who will be moving into their new home in a week. Their furniture is only stored in the rooms, which gives the interior of the house a somewhat crowded impression.

Nevertheless, we like the house right away, especially the living room. It is spacious, has large windows on both sides, a newly fitted carpet, and wooden beams, and the gas fire is surrounded by red brick walls. All this exudes a country house idyll. The kitchen is also spacious and fully equipped. A cooker, refrigerator, and even a washing machine are available. Everything is perfect for us! On the upper floor, there are three bedrooms plus a bathroom. A medium-sized garden extends behind the house, which is adjoined by a meadow. The windows on the ground floor are double-glazed, whereby unfortunately there are sliding windows on the upper floor. The house has central heating in addition to a gas fire in the living room. We like what we see and have both already decided to rent this country house if possible.

After the first tour of the house, the landlady appears. She lives only a short distance away and is young and friendly. Since we've already viewed the house and don't want to disturb the current tenants any further, we decided to go to her house to discuss further details. We learn that she is not the actual owner of the house, but her sister who is currently working as a nurse in the Middle East. When I asked how long we could rent the house for, I was told that the sister probably wouldn't be returning to Britain any time soon and that we could rent the house for a few years. We let the woman know that we are interested in a period of up to three years and she confirms that this shouldn't be a problem.

The discussion shifts to the rental price, and we are told that it costs £272 a month, which isn't exactly cheap although this amount includes the rates plus water while we would have to pay for gas and electricity ourselves. While it is not a bargain, with two salaries it should be affordable. Since both the house and the area appeal to us, we don't hesitate, especially since we learn that other people are also interested in this rental property. We have to make a quick decision, which we do, and explain that we definitely want to rent the house. The only issue to be clarified is when we can move in. "Mid-February", is the answer. The current tenants' new house should be ready for occupancy by then. Everything seems perfect. Seems! As is so often the case with quick decisions, everything is wonderful at the beginning but then doubts arise.

A few days later, we reviewed the rental price. We were so excited about the house and especially worried that someone else might snatch it away from us, that we hadn't thought about the rent in detail. We suddenly realize how expensive the house really is at £272 a month. In comparison, we are currently paying just £88 a month for our two-bedroom flat in Duffield. The house in Blackbrook would cost more than three times our current rent in addition to the running costs. Can we afford this? What we pay for rent we cannot spend elsewhere. Do we want that? Suddenly, we have doubts. On the one hand, we have already expressed a firm commitment, on the other hand, there may be houses available at a reduced rate. Wouldn't it be better to continue searching? We think back and forth, end up not knowing what to do, and try to calm ourselves. Finally, we decided that I should return to the landlady to talk about the rent again and that's how we proceed.

The next evening, I visited the landlady again. She admits that the rent is expensive, but we don't have to take the house if it's too much for us. I definitely don't want to make a mistake now because we really like the house, especially the wonderful location in the countryside. We can rent the house at the agreed price because we were the first prospective tenants to express our interest. However, if we don't want it anymore, other interested parties are already waiting for whom the rental price is not too expensive. These are the facts.

I return home. Now that we know that there is no obligation to rent the house if the price seems too expensive for us, and above all that other interested parties also want to rent the property, our doubts fade. Hopefully, we haven't gambled away the landlady's willingness to let us have the house because of our concerns. Maybe she's currently thinking about giving it to someone else. Our heads are spinning. Why did we start all this doubting? It leads to nothing. Can we afford the house or not? That is now the all-important question. We have to react quickly and carefully review our current salaries. The rent is expensive, but after rational consideration, we decide that we can afford it. The fact that we both like the house and the surroundings significantly influences this decision.

In order not to take any risks, I returned once more to the landlady to tell her that we had now thought about it carefully and would like to rent the house at the price she had quoted. Although the woman is a little surprised to see me again on the same night, she assures me that we can rent the house as discussed on Sunday. What excitement! We almost destroyed this great opportunity just because we suddenly became scared. Luckily, we managed to get things under control.

To be able to live so far out in the country we need a second car as I will have to drive around thirty-six kilometres from Blackbrook to work at the East Midlands airport and back every day, while Marie also requires a car to get to her workplace in Duffield.

Hence, we start studying the adverts for second-hand cars again. I find a reasonably priced Volkswagen Polo, call the owner, and view the vehicle the same evening. The car is in very good condition, and the selling price is £1,000, which is a fair price. We bought the car the same evening, this time without any concerns.

We've been lucky with both of our cars bought in the UK. Apart from a few minor repairs, there were no problems with either vehicle during our entire stay in Britain.

FIRST RENTED HOUSE IN BLACKBROOK, DERBYSHIRE

We gave notice on our flat in Duffield. However, moving into our new home, which was planned for mid-February, is slightly delayed as the elderly couple's new house is not yet ready for occupancy. This is unfavourable since we have already given notice on our flat but we are assured that the removal should only be delayed by a week. Hopefully, this proves to be correct because if not, the situation will be challenging. However, the schedule can be met, and everything goes well. On Saturday, February 21st, we can finally move into our lovely country house.

I had previously taken three days off and completely repainted the rooms on the first floor. A touch of colour can change so much - everything immediately becomes brighter, fresher, and cleaner.

On our moving day, we rent a van and friends help us. The more help, the faster it goes. Now we have an entire house and garden to ourselves in beautiful surroundings.

As is the case after every move, we don't sleep very well during the first night in a new environment. Everything is still unfamiliar, and new noises surround us. Something cracks or rustles somewhere, outside in the darkness a small owl calls for hours. We live far out in the country now and it's pitch-dark behind the house. Wherever we've lived in recent years, our domicile has always been in a residential area that was well-lit at night. The road to Ashbourne runs in front of the house and is only dimly lit at night and it's almost completely dark and silent here. This complete silence is particularly eerie during our first night, as it is only occasionally interrupted by the calls of a small owl.

We lie in bed, tired from moving, but wide awake. We long for our familiar surroundings. However, in our previous accommodations, we also had the experience of the first night with unfamiliar sounds and, after that, things slowly became more familiar. Now it will certainly be the same again. The hours passed, the small owl stopped calling, and the silence became absolute. Eventually, we fell asleep, our first night in Blackbrook.

After a few weeks, we've settled in. The complete darkness of the night no longer disturbs us, and the peace and quiet behind the house is marvellous.

Our new home is fairly spacious. The large living room and the kitchen are on the ground floor, while the first floor features two large bedrooms, one small bedroom, and a bathroom. The back garden is bordered by a brook. This is probably the most interesting aspect of this garden, namely that we have our own strip of flowing water. There is also a small shed with garden tools, a lawn, an apple tree, and space for planting vegetables. In front of the house, there is a front garden with grass, flowers, and bushes, and next to the kitchen, there is a carport for one vehicle. The second car can be parked right in front of the house.

On the first floor, we choose the room with a view of the garden as our bedroom. Our double bed, chest of drawers, and cupboard look great in this freshly painted room. The view over the garden to the meadow behind the brook, where a few cows frequently graze, especially in summer, is gorgeous. Meadows are bordered by hedges, mighty trees, and a mountain ridge with sheep grazing on its green slopes. What an inspiring and peaceful sight! I often stand at this window and look out at the mountain ridge. The world, with all its hustle and bustle and restlessness, lies ahead of this ridge. I am behind it, in a picturesque valley, safe and secure in the heart of England.

A haulier lives with his family in the semi next door and we get to know them fairly quickly.

A total of seven houses are lined up along the country road, while further buildings stretch along a side street. There are no shops up here, and we have to go down to Belper to do our shopping.

We also get to know the other direct neighbours. In such a small community, everyone naturally wants to know who has just moved in as quickly as possible. Our new neighbours are very friendly and helpful, and after just a few weeks we feel right at home here.

Thus, this new project was successfully completed. We've changed our residence, moved to a house in the countryside, and bought a second car. So far, everything went well.

Concerning my occupation, a higher salary also means more work. In addition to my translation tasks, I am supposed to set up and manage a customer database on a computer. For this purpose, I have to work closely with the sales engineers. My new job title is Technical Support Engineer, and, whatever that means, I like the job.

In addition to managing the database, I mainly translate enquiries, specification sheets, and all other correspondence in German, call customers and business partners in Germany, Austria, and Switzerland and take care of all sorts of other tasks if urgently required. I really cannot complain about having too little work.

I get along well with my colleagues. Naturally, as is always the case, there are people with whom one gets along better and that one likes less. It's the same here. As a foreigner, you are teased differently than the locals although I mostly don't mind because it's not meant in a bad way. However, there are days when one is not in a particularly good mood and on such days, it's annoying to be teased although I'm also learning to remain calm in such situations to avoid confrontations. If I, as a foreigner, make the mistake of arguing too intensely with someone, the other colleagues show solidarity with their countryman out of national pride and I suddenly have the whole group against me. This is unpleasant, so I try to avoid it.

At Easter, Marie's sister visits us. She is incredibly lucky with the weather, the sun is shining, the sky is bright blue, and it's hot.

The weather in England can sometimes be a problem. On the Continent, the prevailing opinion is that the climate on the British Isles is fairly fresh, foggy, and wet, which is anything but pleasant. However, this is not always accurate. While it admittedly can happen that it rains more often, especially during the summer months, in spring and autumn one can experience very nice, sometimes even hot, days.

My sister-in-law is pleasantly surprised by so much sun and warmth. Since both Marie and I work during the day, she has to spend some time on her own with walks or bicycle tours. In the evening, she tells us that she rode her bicycle on the left-hand side of the road, as required. She cycled with great concentration, especially on narrow country lanes with relatively low traffic. However, the tendency to drift to the right, as usual, was particularly strong.

In May, we spend a few days with friends in Cumbria in the Lake District National Park. Although we've already heard a lot about the beauty of this area, reality surpasses it all. The landscape with its mountains, forests, and lakes is unique! At this early time of the year, the peaks are still coated with a light blanket of snow. We stay in a B&B in Windermere, walk around a few lakes, climb a mountain, eat comfortably in restaurants, and visit pubs for a pint or two in the evening. It is a relaxing break.

After this short vacation, I have to travel to Germany for a business meeting as one of our measuring machines has been sold to a Swiss company as part of an FMS system (Flexible Manufacturing System). Now all the suppliers are meeting to discuss how to proceed, and especially how to integrate individual components. I accompany our project manager to translate if necessary. These are interesting days.

After this meeting, we fly back to Birmingham but I cannot go home yet as there is an industrial fair at the Birmingham Exhibition Centre, right next to the airport, where we also have a booth. There, I take care of the Customer Database, which means that I enter all the enquiries into the system. In addition, I also take care of German-speaking business partners and visitors who come to our booth. As is usual at trade fairs, there is a business meal on the last evening which is very motivating as one identifies with the company and is proud to be a part of it. After one week, I can finally return home again.

During the following week, I return to Germany to accompany three of our software engineers who want to discuss further integration topics concerning the FMS system with German technicians. Again, I act as a translator. The meeting is also a good opportunity to get to know the employees on the German side as I'm sure I'll be on the phone with them more often later on. Teamwork is always easier if you know each other personally.

We enjoy the relaxing summer months. The weather varies, sometimes it's hot, sometimes wet, sometimes windy, and occasionally it is cold. Marie visits her parents in France during July but returns just in time for my thirty-first birthday. We spend the evening of this special day together in a cosy restaurant in Matlock. A jazz band is playing and the food is excellent.

On the last weekend in July, we spontaneously decide to take a short break, pack the tent into the car, and drive to Skegness on the North Sea coast. Skegness, or "Skeggy" as the locals affectionately call it, is the closest seaside resort to Derby. It is, so to speak, the "Beach of Derby". We've heard a lot about this place, and now we want to experience it for ourselves. As in almost all British seaside resorts, there is also an amusement park here, where we spend some time on Saturday evening. On Sunday morning, we walk along the seafront. The sun is shining, the shops are open, and we stroll around enjoying the sights.

The following weekend, we drive down to Oxford. The venerable university buildings exude a very special flair. One can feel the importance of this university town, in which part of the country's leading elite is trained - it literally "smells" like science and education here.

One week later, we are back in Cambridge and visit our friends. Andrew borrows a punt boat from his college and we spend the afternoon punting on the River Cam, including a picnic on board.

The rest of August we spend at home in Blackbrook.

My cousin, who is currently motorcycling around the UK, took the opportunity to drop by for the weekend. His special motorbike, a "Royal Enfield", is not only admired by us but also by many motorbike enthusiasts in England.

Another family celebration takes place in France in September. Like last year, we took the plane from the East Midlands airport to Paris. It's pretty windy and cool as we leave the UK. One hour and a half later, humid, hot air hits us in Paris. The temperature difference is pretty amazing. We stay in France for a week.

At the end of September, we have a barbecue with friends in our garden in Blackbrook. We grill, enjoy salads, drink wine or beer, and round off the meal with a cake for dessert. What a lovely late summer evening.

On the whole, we spent a wonderful summer at our home in Blackbrook in 1987. The tranquillity and lush nature out here in the countryside are lovely, and the neighbours are ideal. Everyone helps each other.

We often have breakfast on the patio in the bright sunshine. Regarding the garden, we left one half of the backyard as a flower garden and used the other half for planting various vegetables including tomatoes, carrots, radishes, beetroots, onions, green beans, and lettuce, whereby we only had real success with the lettuce which thrives and tastes delicious. With the remaining vegetables, there is only moderate or no success. The carrots fall victim to rabbits and mice, the tomatoes only sparsely turn red, the radishes also disappear into some animal stomachs, and some of the onions rot in the damp soil. However, we can at least celebrate moderate success with the beetroots and the green beans.

A brook in the garden naturally encourages (not only children) to build a dam - one can't just watch the water flow, one has to restrain it. My first attempts fail miserably. Either the water penetrates the dam, or the floods tear down the entire structure after a short period.

However, one day I managed to create a little masterpiece. I dam up the brook and the entire construction withstands. Days go by, and I've long since forgotten my best achievement in construction when one evening the doorbell rings. I open the door and look into my neighbour's smiling face. We know each other well. He's not upset but asks me to tear down "the masterpiece of German engineering" because the water is already backing up into his garden. I instantly remember the dam construction project. The heavy rain of the last few days has caused the brook to swell considerably. Normally, such masses of water would have immediately demolished earlier attempts to build a dam. However, this masterpiece withstands! I hurry to the end of the garden and discover the disaster right away. It really is high time to remove the stones to allow the flooding to drain off. Nevertheless, I'm a bit proud that this dam resisted so well.

During the summer months, it is pretty calm at work. There are no business trips planned and my workload is limited to maintaining the database plus some translation work. However, that's enough to keep me busy, and I don't get bored.

I especially like to structure the database as all important information has to be retrieved quickly. Weekly sales meetings are held to discuss what information should be included in the database and I am then tasked with implementing what was agreed on, which is very creative work.

At the beginning of October, things become hectic. The end of the financial year is approaching, the sales figures are not yet satisfying, and attempts are made to secure more orders. The atmosphere in the office becomes more tense. Unfortunately, as a foreigner, I'm the weakest member of the team and have to serve as an outlet from time to time when some colleagues think they need to vent their frustration. In this context, allusions to my native country are not uncommon and I usually shrug them off. However, my job is also becoming more stressful. Due to all the extra work, the regular tasks are almost impossible to cope with. Something is still missing, something else doesn't fit. "Why isn't that finished yet?" "Maybe because something else had to be done in addition?" That's how it is every day now. The level of excitement increases proportionately to the stress. My colleagues have an outlet, but I don't. I wish I could react promptly and purposefully to most of the things that are thrown at me but in a foreign language that is not always as easy as in your mother tongue.

I find myself slipping into a personal crisis. Suddenly, the negative comments affect me personally - they no longer bounce off me but go deeper. Antipathy arises. I don't show anything if a comment hurts me because I don't want others to have the additional satisfaction of seeihg my discomfort. However, it annoys me more and more every day. Who actually gives the English the right to judge other countries in such an arrogant way? What are they so proud of? Their former empire that no longer exists? Their language, which everyone has to learn because it is the universal language? Their royal family? Their left-hand traffic? What actually?

I am in a crisis! Privately, I still like the country and its people, but professionally things are no longer optimal.

In November, I seriously considered terminating our stay in Britain earlier than planned. I'll soon complete the second year of my current job. Due to my current frustration, I'm not sure whether I will be able to work with this company for a third year and thus my fourth year in the UK. During the next few months, I suddenly find myself struggling to reach the end of the year without quitting.

The crisis at work continues, and sometimes I just want to leave. Every day I have to motivate myself to cope with the excess workload in addition to my regular job. Every week that goes by is a personal achievement. The end of the year is approaching and I haven't given up yet.

However, the last two months of 1987 are not that bad after all. A happy event is announced privately, we are having a child! At the end of November, it is certain that Marie is pregnant. Our first child is due to be born at the end of July next year. Where will we live then? However, for now, we don't worry about these details but simply look forward to welcoming our first child.

At the end of November, the annual Christmas Dinner Dance of the building society where Marie works takes place. There is a delicious buffet, raffle tickets are sold, and we dance till after midnight.

At the beginning of December, we intend to spend a weekend in London and book a hotel room. We've been looking forward to this short break for weeks, and it unexpectedly turns out to be even better than planned.

A Swiss engineer, whose company bought one of our measuring machines that must now be technically approved, has been in our factory for a few days. Unfortunately, there are some problems which means the customer has to come back in about two weeks. Since I've looked after this engineer to support him with any language problems, I'm also invited to lunch at a restaurant. The current situation is not ideal for either side. The engineer has to fly home without approval and has to return later on. We have to admit mistakes and cannot meet the promised delivery date. To be able to make something positive out of the whole situation, my boss would like to fulfil the customer's personal wish, namely to spend a weekend in London. During lunch, I was asked if I could accompany him to London. Since I was planning to do this privately anyway, my boss offered me the opportunity to accompany our guest to London that evening and to take my wife with me. There, we should have dinner together, and he would book a table for three in a very good restaurant. In addition, the company will pay for the additional overnight stay. I like the offer! The evening in London turns out to be one of those experiences that one won't forget for the rest of one's life.

We meet the Swiss engineer at 6 p.m. at Derby train station and board the Intercity train to London. On arrival, we take a taxi, drive a short distance to our hotel, and then head straight on to the restaurant where a table has been booked for us. On the way, we pass through the brightly lit streets of the British capital. It's like a dream!

We enjoy this special evening to the fullest. Accompanied by soft piano music, we first treat ourselves to an aperitif and choose the main course plus wine. After a while, we are led to a table set for three people. The plates bear the restaurant's emblem and the atmosphere is fantastic. All three of us chose asparagus as a starter. When it comes to the main course, the tastes differ. Marie chooses a tender steak, our guest a spicy pepper steak, and I choose salmon. We enjoy French red wine with it. At the end of the feast, we think that strawberries would be perfect for dessert, and order them. Finally, we receive a chocolate truffle and Marie is given a red rose from a huge bouquet. We dine excellently, drink very good wine, and have pleasant conversations. The engineer, a very friendly man, always wanted to visit London. He's pleased, we're happy, and all in all, it is a wonderful unforgettable evening. For a few hours, we find ourselves in another world. Privately we could never have afforded a meal in such an exquisite restaurant. I realize that when I see the bill. It's astronomical! However, I don't have to pay for it as my company handles it. We take a taxi back to the hotel through the illuminated streets of this cosmopolitan metropolis. All three of us agree that we won't forget this evening.

On Saturday morning, we take our guest on a city tour and manage to secure the services of an extremely accommodating taxi driver who not only drives us around but also tells us interesting facts about places of interest. For lunch, we visit the "Swiss House" at Leicester Square, which is probably the most obvious thing to do when looking after a guest from Switzerland. Then, it's time to say goodbye, as the engineer has to go to the airport.

The business part of our stay in London is over, and now the private part begins. Today's evening meal will not be as exquisite as the feast last night. However, we dine well and then take a taxi to Harrods, the world-famous department store. You just have to see it once. We don't buy anything, just look around.

On Sunday, we take a leisurely stroll through the streets and squares, sit down on a park bench, and immerse ourselves in London's atmosphere. What a lively city, rich in history, with its many parks and the black taxis and red double-decker buses naturally contributing to its special flair. In the late afternoon, an Intercity train takes us back to Derby in around two hours.

When I return home on one of the following evenings, I immediately notice that something is wrong. Marie shows me a letter from a lawyer. I read it through, and am also taken aback. Our landlady's lawyer informs us that the owner of the house plans to return to the UK in July and would like to move in again. According to the lawyer, our tenancy is limited to one year only and will therefore expire in February. However, should we wish, we could stay until early July.

This is a nasty shock! It is the first time that I've heard of a time limit concerning our tenancy agreement. Before I rented the house, I explicitly stated that we were not interested in a short rental period but intended to rent the house for at least two years. Moreover, the sister of the house owner didn't even want to set up a tenancy agreement. However, I insisted on one at the time because what I have in writing provides safety.

I immediately pick up the tenancy agreement and read it through. To be on the safe side, I went through it a second time but could not find any limit concerning the rental period. Somehow there must be some kind of misunderstanding here, as otherwise, the whole issue is simply inexplicable.

However, we are cautious and want to have the details checked more closely. Fortunately, there is a lawyer in our circle of friends whom we ask for advice. He also peruses the rental contract and reassures us. First of all, this tenancy agreement is not even complete and secondly, there is no time limit at all. We are completely safe. If we want to stay in the house, nothing can happen to us. He promises to write to the opposing lawyer, highlighting the incompleteness of the rental contract and explaining our intention to stay on.

We are reassured as we know that we don't have to leave if we don't want to. The opposite side is now also informed that we have a legal adviser and will not be intimidated. It's always good to have a lawyer in one's circle of friends.

Friday, December 18th. Today is my last working day for this year since I'll be on Christmas vacation starting tomorrow. I feel like a winner, as I persevered and didn't quit my job despite the stress and frustration. Two years working for a company in the UK are now part of my work experience. The hectic rush at the end of the year is over and I know from experience that the first few months of the new year will be much calmer. I'm slowly beginning to believe that I might still be able to complete the third year.

Marie is spending the Christmas holidays in France, while I am going to Germany.

Back in Derbyshire again, we celebrate New Year's Eve together with our friends Jean and Ian in our house in Blackbrook. As the end of the year approaches, Ian wants to show us a New Year's Eve tradition from his native Scotland. Shortly before midnight, he hands me a piece of fruit cake with which I have to leave the house and must not return until after midnight.

Hence, I find myself standing in front of the house, surrounded by absolute silence and with only the moonlight illuminating the rolling hills all around. At this moment, I feel a deep inner peace and gratitude. The past year, which will end in a few minutes, was sometimes difficult – mainly as far as the job was concerned – but overall, it was successful. We are still doing well and live in a pleasant house amid a beautiful landscape. I often remember those last minutes of 1987, standing content and proud in front of our house in Blackbrook on that quiet, bright New Year's Eve.

I look at my watch. It's already past midnight, and 1988 has begun. Time to return to the house where the others are already waiting. The fruitcake, I learn, symbolises the happiness that is brought into the house with the new year. Let's hope it works! We eat the cake, drink whiskey, and continue chatting for a while. Then it's time to say goodbye because we're all very tired. The new year will bring us a joyful event, namely the birth of our first child. We are both looking forward to it.

While the first days of 1988 bring some snow, the white splendour doesn't last long.

In mid-January, we receive a letter from our lawyer with a copy of his written communication to the other party's legal advisor. According to the tenancy agreement, we can stay in the house for as long as we want.

A few weeks later, we received an unexpected call. The owner of the house, that means the sister of the local landlady, is on the phone. She is currently in the UK and would like to come around one evening. Why not? A clarifying discussion would certainly also be reasonable for us. I agree, but I'm sure that she won't come on her own, and I turn out to be right.

She appears together with her partner. Both are returning from a skiing holiday in the US and, after a brief stopover in the UK, will be returning to the Middle East where they are currently working. The only topic for tonight is the tenancy and they instantly try to intimidate us. However, I'm well prepared for it. Thanks to the information from our lawyer, I remain perfectly calm. The woman is nervous and strained, and she often scratches her chin. Her partner, on the other hand, is calmer and starts the conversation. Both are currently working in the Middle East, their employment contracts run until July of this year, but will not be renewed after that. Therefore, they have to return to the UK. They don't yet know whether they want to move into the house themselves or sell it. That's the job situation.

Now we talk about the tenancy agreement. It should have been limited to one year, which the sister, the local landlady, unfortunately, forgot to include in the agreement. Above all, the document is incomplete. I reply that it is not my job to evaluate this issue, that is my lawyer's responsibility. This impresses both of them and they realize that we are not afraid at all.

Now we explain our point of view. A year ago, we only rented the house because there was no time limit. In addition, we made it clear when we signed the tenancy agreement that we wanted to rent the house for at least two years. This did not appear to have been a problem at the time the agreement was signed. If the sister didn't draft the document correctly, that's not our problem. There is only one tenancy agreement and that is in our favour. We are also expecting a child. Mainly for this reason we cannot and do not want to leave the house in July.

Now they want to see the tenancy agreement, which I expected. However, I think it wiser not to give away our only piece of evidence and I tell them, "The document is currently with my lawyer." I can see the disappointment on their faces. They would have gladly taken the document away from me, which they considered to be incomplete. But this did not work. I'm not handing over the agreement. Besides, they probably already have a copy of it.

Throughout the entire conversation, I stay completely calm and relaxed, while the other parties act extremely nervous. After an hour and a half, the two leave us again. We have clearly communicated our positions and behaved in a civilised manner. It is now up to the lawyers to investigate further. We should be fine. The opposite side has to pay their legal advisor, while fortunately, we don't.

After a week, we receive a letter from our landlady's lawyer informing us that under certain conditions, she is willing to let us have the house for another two years. However, we have to sign a new temporary agreement and the monthly rent will increase. I immediately consult my lawyer. He advises me not to sign anything, because legally we are absolutely safe with our current tenancy agreement. Why should we worsen our current situation when we don't have to? We neither sign a new agreement nor accept a rent increase because the rent is already expensive enough.

Further weeks pass. For some time, I've noticed a wet spot on the wall next to the front door, which seems to be expanding. Moisture must penetrate the masonry from the outside and something needs to be done to prevent the damage from getting worse. At least the landlady should be aware of it. On the advice of my lawyer, I write a letter informing them of the damage.

Sunday, January 31st. It is a pleasant, sunny day. We go for a walk in the near vicinity and return home around 4 p.m. Recently, some mail has arrived for the sister of the house owner, who herself lived in our current house some time ago. A parcel is also included this time. She lives just a few yards down the road, and I should take her the items as maybe they are important. Moreover, as I haven't seen her since the matter with the lawyer, I might as well use this brief visit to test the mood.

Hence, I decided that tonight I would pay her a visit. Even though I cannot deny a slight feeling of apprehension, I'm not a coward and, anyway, I'm right! I thus grab the letters and the parcel and set off. After a short walk, I reach her house and knock on the door. First of all, nothing happens. I knock again. It takes a while, then a face appears at the kitchen window. Shortly thereafter, the landlady's sister opens the door. From her facial expression, I immediately recognise that she is in a bad mood. I handed over the mail and would like to briefly mention the damp spot on the wall but can't get that far.

While the confrontation wasn't unexpected, I underestimated the intensity. She explains that I am a very bad person who would destroy her family because her sister no longer speaks to her due to the incomplete tenancy agreement. I would have known exactly that she wanted to limit the tenancy to just one year, but unfortunately failed to mention this in writing. I would now shamefully exploit this error. She insults me as an impostor, a criminal, generally as a very bad person. I am speechless. From time to time, I try to counter her arguments because what she says is simply not true. However, she doesn't even let me respond. Her sister, she continues, wants to get married next year but cannot do this because we do not want to move out of her house. Hence, this is also our fault.

It keeps getting worse. Of course, she says, I would be fine now, since nothing could happen to me legally due to her mistake. This seems to annoy her the most. She hopes that I won't be able to sleep peacefully at night. More accusations follow.

After she has calmed down a bit, I try to explain the situation from my point of view. However, a reasonable discussion is not possible here at the front door, as she only sees things from her perspective. Again and again, she insults me and becomes increasingly angry. At one point, I even consider it wiser to take a step back so as not to be standing right on the doorstep. A short distance would be advisable because she is becoming more and more furious, and one never knows what can happen next. I just hope she doesn't completely lose control.

Now her husband also appears and I don't know how he will react. I have no desire to risk a fierce row, especially as I have had enough of the unjustified accusations and insults. A reasonable exchange of arguments is not possible here. Time to go before I get in real trouble because I'm alone and have no witnesses.

Finally, she slams the door in my face.

Here I am, totally surprised! And I just wanted to deliver the mail.

I slowly walk back home and wonder what she meant when she said she hoped I wouldn't be able to sleep peacefully at night. Was that supposed to be a threat? You never know what's going on in some people's minds. If I had known what to expect, I wouldn't have gone to see her. But it's too late now.

I'm angry because I do not deserve such insults and insinuations. There was never any talk of a limited tenancy. We have kept the house in good condition and even improved it by repainting the rooms at our own expense. We also looked after the garden, never caused any problems, and always paid the rent on time. Just because the landlady's sister made a mistake we are supposed to be bad people?

Suddenly, we don't feel like staying here any longer. Why should we take care of everything and pay the high rent when we're just taken for mean impostors? Can we still feel safe here? If someone wants revenge on us, it's very lonely and dark out here at night. We only know the immediate neighbours who are on our side. But the landlady's sister grew up here and knows many more residents that she could incite against us. The calm, content and, above all, peaceful life in the countryside is most likely to be over.

Our mood on this Sunday evening tends towards zero. If we have to move again, then back to our own country. However, that's easier said than done. First, I would have to find a new job.

Suddenly, we find ourselves in the middle of a fundamental crisis. In such a situation it's good to have friends with whom one can discuss problems. We ask Jean and Ian to come and see us and we discuss the incident with them. The legal situation is clear. We can stay in the house as long as we want. However, do we still want that? The personal relationship with the landlady's sister is poisoned. I don't think we can feel comfortable here anymore. Something has been irrevocably destroyed by the whole incident, and that's the peace we found here in this beautiful valley. Above all, I have concerns that someone might try to make life difficult for us out of revenge. Fortunately, our friends are with us and tell us their opinions. We begin to approach the whole issue more objectively and calmly, and not as emotionally as at the beginning.

There is another property that we might be able to rent. The company I work for has rented a house for six months for a foreign colleague who is being trained in the UK. This colleague currently lives there with his wife, and the rental property is not far from where I work. The six months will be over in a few weeks, after which this house could be rented again. I would have to ask the landlord if that was the case.

The very next day I contacted him and he informed me that as soon as the colleague moved out at the end of February, the house would be free and could be rented again. The rental price is £240 per month exclusive additional charges and around £300 per month inclusive charges. I arrange an appointment to view the house. My colleague even invites us to dinner. While the house makes a good impression, it has no central heating and a few old electric heaters provide warmth. This is not ideal, especially since we've gotten used to the central heating in our current domicile and don't want to miss it anymore. Moreover, by next winter we'll have a child who needs warmth. Such a high rental price should offer a little more comfort.

A few days later, I learned that the house of a colleague who was transferred to the US for work is available to rent. The owner would like to let it to a trustworthy person while he's away. As an employee of the same company, I would have a good chance of renting the house. I only know the man superficially as he worked as a technician in the factory and has been in the US for two months now. I am told that I should call him if I'm interested. I do this and realize that it would also be in his interest if I rented his house. It is located in Melbourne, south of Derby. The monthly rent would be just £180 exclusive additional costs, virtually a special price among colleagues. Naturally, this is very convenient for us. However, he would rent out the house for one year only, as that's how long he intends to stay in the US and he subsequently plans to return to the UK and wants to move into his house again. I think we should take a closer look at the house. After the viewing, we can always talk about details.

The following weekend, we drove to Melbourne and looked at the house. It is relatively new, situated in a quiet residential area on the outskirts of the village, and has central heating, a double garage, and a medium-sized garden. The living room is furnished, the kitchen fully equipped, and there is a washing machine and a television set. We like it immediately. The rental price is a bargain, and only the time limit would be a disadvantage.

We have to think about it. What are our plans for the future? It is now February 1988. In January 1989, I shall have worked for my current employer for three years and lived in the UK for four years. After this period, we wanted to return to Germany anyway. I intended to apply for a job in my own country starting in January 1989. However, I don't know how soon I will be able to find work. The new rental property would be available to us until March 1989. Would that be long enough?

We consider this option and develop a plan. If I start applying for a job in Germany this autumn, I should most likely have found something suitable by the spring of next year. This is certainly an ambitious plan but it should be feasible. Hence, we could leave the UK by March 1989 at the latest and the limited rental period wouldn't be a problem. This seems to be an ideal solution. We could get a modern house for little money and the annoying legal dispute would be over.

We decide quickly. I called my colleague and told him that we would like to rent his house for a year. It's a good solution for both sides. He tells us that we could move in whenever we wanted, the key is with the neighbours. Perfect!

During the last two weeks of February, we once again packed up all our belongings and informed the homeowner's lawyer that we would be moving out at the end of February. We don't keep a notice period, since it was claimed that the rental contract only lasts until the end of February anyway. Hence, the matter is settled for us.

Our direct neighbours regret our departure. However, we're not completely out of sight yet, are not moving too far away, and we can still keep in touch.

SECOND RENTED HOUSE IN MELBOURNE, DERBYSHIRE

Saturday, February 27th. At 10 a.m. we're ready to go after a final tour of the empty rooms that have been our home for a year. For one summer, we were very happy here and now it's time to look ahead. What's over is over. It was nice, but now a new phase of life begins.

I deliver the front door key because I'm curious to see if I'll meet the woman one last time who slammed the door in my face just a few weeks ago. However, one of her children shows up and takes the key. With that done, this last formality is also completed. We certainly would have wished for a nicer ending but we cannot influence that anymore.

I get behind the steering wheel of the rented van, start the engine, and drive towards the future. What an intense feeling of freedom driving down the road with all our belongings in the back of the van, not being tied to anything.

We need almost half an hour for the approximately thirty kilometres between the two places. Once in Melbourne, we unload everything with the help of friends and place most of it in the double garage. We only assemble our bedroom furniture and some wooden shelves, because the house is fully furnished. Luckily there is a double garage, where else would we have placed all our additional furniture?

As always in new surroundings, we don't sleep deeply during the first night. From our country life, we are now used to complete silence at night, apart from the calls of an owl. There was no road or other buildings behind our house in Blackbrook, and only a mountain with trees and hedges. Here, the street now runs directly below the bedroom window, and there are street lights and many other houses. Today is Saturday, and many residents return home late, cars pass, and there is a lot of activity on the pavement. However, after a few weeks, we were already used to all the new sounds and conditions.

Gradually, we set up our new home. Apart from the immediate neighbours, we don't get to know anyone. There is no comparison to the small community we just came from, with only a few residents, but a very close neighbourhood. The people there were interested in us because we were part of their community. Here in our new neighbourhood people are constantly moving in and out. Nobody really cares very much who lives here. Since we will only be staying for one year anyway, this doesn't bother us. We have enough friends and don't need more.

After just a few weeks, we are settled in. Like the previous one, the new house is a semi. The outside walls are partly decorated with red bricks, there is no cellar, and the double garage offers sufficient storage space. The kitchen and living room are on the ground floor, and there are two large bedrooms, a small children's room, and a bathroom on the first floor. The living room is fully furnished with a wooden dining table, four matching chairs, two armchairs, and a sofa. We add two wooden shelves and our stereo system, use one of the two bedrooms as a guest room, empty the other one and deploy our double bed there. The small room will be the children's room, as our baby is supposed to be born at the end of July.

Unfortunately, we soon found out that our new residential area is directly in the flight corridor of the East Midlands airport, which is located only a few kilometres to the east. Cargo planes thunder over us at night, and during the summer months, there are charter flights as well. Surprisingly, we get used to all of this noise very quickly, and we only occasionally wake up when a particularly loud "bird" passes over us. What a difference to the silent nights in our valley on the edge of the mountains!

I often think back to Blackbrook, especially to those late summer evenings when I strolled through the garden, stopped by the brook, and listened to the silence. Only the soft gurgling of the brook could be heard. Sometimes a train rattled through the twilight in the distance, now and then vehicles passed the road in front of the house, which a few old street lights tried to illuminate. Behind it, the world seemed to have come to an end. The only light in our house shimmered faintly through the curtains of the bedroom window. These were moments of deep peace that I haven't felt since we left Blackbrook. It was probably due to the remoteness of the place, the ideal neighbourhood, or just because it was all very special.

March 11th marks the third anniversary of my arrival in the UK and we celebrate this special event with Irene and John at our home in Melbourne. We owe them so much. They gave me a great deal of support, especially during the first crucial weeks. Through them, I obtained my first flat in Duffield. They were also the ones we could always rely on. Just the feeling of knowing that their door was always open gave me the strength and courage to assert myself in a foreign country. I never felt alone, was rarely homesick, and felt safe and secure. I owe that mainly to these two people. We still have a very special friendship.

At Easter, we spend a few days in the Cotswolds. This magnificent landscape stretches out to the west of London between Oxford and Cheltenham and comprises gentle hills, green meadows and pastures, and picturesque villages with cosy stone cottages. We've booked a room in a B&B and feel extremely comfortable.

At the end of April, I attend a seminar in Bavaria. Two days after my return, I have to leave again. This time I'm travelling to an industrial trade fair in Stuttgart which gives me the opportunity to explore the surroundings during my spare time. We secretly consider Stuttgart as a suitable destination for our return to Germany as the countryside is pleasant, France is not far away, and there are many interesting industrial companies in the region.

A few weeks ago, I wrote to the Chamber of Industry and Commerce in Stuttgart and asked for information and addresses of local companies. The first step towards planning and realising our return to Germany has been taken. Based on these documents, I created a preferred list of companies I would like to work for. Thus, it is an advantage that the trade fair is taking place in Stuttgart.

The next three months comprise a sort of exploration and information stage. During this time, I intend to collect as much information as possible and evaluate it and, once I have done so, I intend to apply for suitable positions.

I return home on Saturday, May 7th, but only see Marie very briefly as she will be travelling to her parents in France on the next day.

While she's away, I start to write down the experiences of the last three years. Whether it will ever become a book remains to be seen. I write the first page on the 9th of May. At this time, I don't know how the story will end. In particular, I am thinking of our first child, who will be born in about three months. When it is older, it should be able to read for itself what its parents experienced before and at the time of its birth.

I contact approximately sixty companies in the Stuttgart area requesting a company profile in addition to some product information. Sixty letters mean a lot of mail charges, an investment that should be worth it. The weeks go by and answers arrive. I'm pleasantly surprised. Although not all companies respond, a response rate of around 90% is quite a success. Based on the extensive information material, I can now assess the companies more realistically.

I'm targeting a position in foreign trade in which I can use both my foreign language skills and international experience. Four years' work experience in Britain should be an advantage for securing this objective.

In early June, we spend a week on holiday in Wales on a farm near Criccieth. We go on day trips, visit famous castles, hike in the mountains, walk along beaches, and admire picturesque places. Wales delights us with forests, high mountains, dark lakes, and a blue-green sea.

Marie is eight months pregnant now, and one can clearly see it.

A cousin from France is visiting us in June. Since it is her first trip to the UK, we've come up with something special for the weekend. We want to take her to London for the day. On Saturday, June 11th, we take a train from Derby to London. On arrival, we get a taxi and ask the driver to get us to Buckingham Palace. He looks at us in astonishment and remarks that he will try to drive as close to the palace as possible. But he won't quite make it today. "Why not?" we ask in surprise. The clarification follows promptly. The annual military parade "Trooping the Colour" in honour of the Queen's birthday takes place today. We didn't think of that. What a coincidence! What luck especially for our visitor! It's her first time in Britain, her first visit to London, and she already has a chance to see the Queen. That's something very special!

Although "The Mall" is crowded with spectators, we managed to find a good site to admire the magnificent carriages of the Royal Family. It's worth the wait. For a brief moment, we see the Queen and some other members of the Royal Family.

After that, we avoid the crowds, relax, and enjoy another tour in one of the typical black taxis. In the evening, we take a train back to Derby and are all very pleased with how the day unfolded.

We are now eagerly awaiting the birth of our first child at Derby City Hospital. Many women from our circle of friends gave birth there and were very satisfied. Our due date is July 25th and the closer it gets, the more impatient we become.

The documentary "Having a Baby" is shown on TV and we follow it with interest.

The weeks in July pass, and there are still no contractions. July 16th is my birthday and we were secretly speculating that the two birthdays might coincide. However, there were no contractions on that day either. We celebrate my birthday at a restaurant near Nottingham. On July 25th, there are still no contractions. We're already past the predetermined date. I now start calling from work every day, but the answer is always "no contractions". When does it finally start? A colleague whose wife recently gave birth advises us to walk a lot as long walks apparently induce contractions.

THE BIRTH OF OUR FIRST DAUGHTER AT DERBY CITY HOSPITAL

On Friday, July 29th, we walk along Staunton Harold Reservoir. However, even after this walk, there are still no contractions.

On Saturday, July 30th, we take another long walk at Calke Abbey Park during the afternoon. Once we get home, we have dinner and finally, around 9 p.m., something finally happens - the first contractions begin. I called the family doctor, he notified the hospital, and we set off and arrived at the hospital around 10 p.m. There, they called us "The United Nations". It certainly doesn't happen every day that a French woman with a German husband gives birth to a child in Great Britain.

After eleven hours, on the morning of July 31, 1988, around 9 a.m., our first child is finally born. A little late, but healthy. At first, I didn't pay attention to the gender of the child, and I'm just glad that it's healthy. It is only after the conversation with a midwife that I find out that it's a girl. I am overjoyed, as we both secretly wanted a daughter. After the child has been breastfed and washed, I can now hold my daughter in my arms for the first time. I'm incredibly proud! She's so beautiful! We call her Rebecca because this name is pronounced almost the same in the three countries she is connected to.

Mother and child stay in the hospital for a week, where I visit them every evening. Fathers can stay as long as they want, which is very nice. I'm almost always the last father to leave at around 11 p.m.

I fetch my wife and daughter from the hospital on Friday, August 5th. Everything is prepared at home. During the next few days and nights, we have to get used to our new role as parents, which requires us to acquire some new skills. However, as time goes by, we become more confident and soon get used to it.

At the Derby Registration Office, I have Rebecca entered into the register of births and received one birth certificate. Additional birth certificates are subject to a fee and I order five more original birth certificates because who knows where we will live in the future.

Now we have to clarify which nationalities our daughter will get. I contacted the German consulate in Liverpool and Marie made enquiries at the French consulate. It doesn't take long before we get an answer. Due to having a German father, Rebecca automatically receives German citizenship. With a French mother, French citizenship is also not a problem.

However, the question arises whether she also qualifies for British citizenship as a result of being born in the UK. We write to the Home Office in London and get in touch with the MEP (Member of the European Parliament) for Derbyshire. Unfortunately, the MEP cannot give us a quick answer in this regard but he promises to take care of it. Since we haven't heard anything for a long time, neither from the Home Office nor from the MEP, we again consulted our friend the lawyer as something concerning this issue may be stipulated in the law. We learn that if Rebecca had been born in the UK before January 1, 1983, she would have automatically been given British citizenship at birth. However, since she was born after this date, this no longer happens automatically. Children born in Great Britain after the first of January 1983 and whose parents are not British nationals only have a right to obtain British citizenship if the parents' residence status can be described as "settled".

Now the question arises as to what exactly "settled" means in this context. Does it mean permanent residence and a permanent job? However, when it comes to British citizenship the law is much more complicated and because of the interpretation of the legal definition of "settled", Rebecca is not able to acquire British citizenship. Generally speaking, we would certainly qualify as being "settled" because we have been in the country for over three years, have a permanent address, a permanent employment contract and, as citizens of the European Union, valid residence permits. However, the lawyers see it differently because although we do have residence permits, these are currently limited to only five years. Hence, due to this time limit, we do not qualify as being "settled" as this definition would only apply to persons with unlimited residence permits. Therefore, Rebecca has no right to British citizenship. However, she already has two nationalities and that's certainly not bad for a start.

By the end of August, I have compiled my application documents. I was able to create a kind of "company hit list" from the information I received and intend to apply for a job starting in September. Everything is prepared, including my CV, letters of application, and copies of certificates.

In September, my parents-in-law from France visited us for two weeks. It is their first crossing of the English Channel. Since they are not used to driving on the left, I take the train to Folkestone on the coast, pick them up and drive them to Melbourne in their car. They are very happy to see their little granddaughter for the first time. Rebecca is now five weeks old.

During their stay, we show them the surrounding countryside. The weather is perfect, the sun shines almost every day, and it is pleasantly warm. I take a few afternoons off for longer tours.

My father-in-law soon developed a particular passion for scones, which are often served with clotted cream and jam. That's no surprise, and we also like scones... if only it weren't for the calories! He also goes shopping every day and, amazingly, comes home with the right products even though he hardly speaks a word of English. Above all, he enjoys pushing his granddaughter around the village in the pram.

At the weekend, friends invite us to lunch. Thus, my parents-in-law also get an insight into an English family.

After two weeks, it is time to say goodbye again. I drive them back to Folkestone and return to Derby by train.

Shortly thereafter, I accompany my boss to Wiesbaden in Germany for a few days where we meet purchasing managers from the Far East who are looking for machine tools in Europe. They also require measuring machines for an FMS system and that's exactly why we meet them, to present our machines and to discuss a possible integration into their FMS system.

I also used this trip to Germany to post some spontaneous letters of application at Frankfurt airport.

The colleague whose house we are currently staying in informs us that he will be staying in the United States a little longer than originally planned. Instead of March, he would now stay until September. Hence, we could stay in his house a few months longer than agreed. Naturally, we are very pleased about this because it reduces the time pressure on us. The first letters of application are in progress, and others will follow at the end of September.

At the beginning of October, my company takes part in an industrial trade fair in Switzerland where I am supposed to take care of visitors who prefer to speak German. Marie uses this time to introduce Rebecca to the family in Germany. We fly to Frankfurt together, hire a car, and drive from there to my parents' house in Bavaria. Rebecca is now two and a half months old, and it's her first flight. She sleeps almost all the time and only becomes restless during the landing. I return to Frankfurt and take the evening flight to Zurich. On the way back, I interrupted the journey again in Frankfurt and spent the weekend with my wife, child, and parents.

We return to Britain on Sunday afternoon. Dense fog prevails during our approach to Birmingham airport. We slowly slide down through a thick veil of clouds. As the grey haze clears, the runway appears directly below us. However, we are still much too high to land. The pilot reacts instantly and pulls the plane up. The airport disappears below us in the dense grey. I'm not the only one with an unpleasant feeling, and the faces of the other travellers also express anxiety. Shortly thereafter, the pilot informs us that he intends to land from the other side, whereby he does not mention whether this is possible. The plane makes a loop and starts a new landing approach. And again we glide through dense fog. It's dead quiet in the cabin. Everyone hopes we hit the runway this time. It works and we are all relieved to have solid ground beneath our feet again.

The first reply to my letters of application arrives in mid-October. Unfortunately, the answer is negative. This is a disappointment. I was convinced that due to my international experience, I would at least be invited to interviews. However, while the company recognises my experience, there unfortunately are no vacancies at present. My optimism receives a slight setback from this - perhaps it won't be that easy to find work back home after all.

By the next day, my self-confidence returns and I prepare further letters of application and send them off. However, during the following days, one negative reply follows the other. I send more letters of application, as no valuable time must be wasted.

At the end of October, I've already sent off twelve letters of application, unfortunately without any success. I couldn't get a single job interview. I have to admit that I didn't expect this. Perhaps I was too optimistic.

I send off more letters of application but only receive rejections. It's never easy to accept setbacks and my confidence is being put to the test. Why am I so uninteresting for companies that operate worldwide and certainly need employees like me? Why don't these companies want to get to know me personally? Performance should pay off. I have something to offer. Why do I only get rejections? What am I doing wrong? Maybe it's because I don't apply to specific job offers, and just randomly. If there are no vacancies, none can be offered to me.

I have to change my strategy and apply to real job advertisements. The sooner the better. However, how do I get job offers from German companies? I would need the Saturday edition of a national newspaper. While no copies of such newspapers are available in either Derby or Nottingham, they should be available at Birmingham airport. On a Saturday morning, I drive to the airport but the journey is in vain. Foreign newspapers always arrive here a few days after their publication date. Hence, this is not the right path to success.

A few days later, I noticed an advertisement in a technical journal for such a national newspaper with an address and telephone number. I rang them up and enquired about the possibility of having the Saturday edition sent to my address in the UK. This is possible. Finally some good news! I subscribe to the Saturday edition, receive it the following Monday, and focus on job advertisements in foreign trade. I don't have to look far either. One company is looking for an export merchant, another one requires an employee for their foreign marketing. For the first time, I start applying for specific job offers. Both companies are based in the Frankfurt/Main area. Every Monday, I now receive a copy of the newspaper, study the job advertisements, choose some of them, and send off one or two letters of application.

Halloween is celebrated on the evening of October 31st. On the way home, I remember just in time to buy some sweets. That evening, our doorbell rings quite often, and the children from the neighbourhood mumble their "trick or treat" and get sweets.

Like every year, November 5th is Bonfire Night. That evening, large bonfires are lit and fireworks light up the evening sky. A long time ago in London, a man named Guy Fawkes wanted to blow up the Houses of Parliament. The gunpowder was already under the building but did not explode because the conspirators were betrayed and the plot was uncovered. Guy Fawkes was arrested and executed. Out of joy that the plot could be prevented, Bonfire Night is still celebrated throughout the UK every first Saturday in November. Straw dolls representing Guy Fawkes are symbolically burned on the bonfires.

On November 16th, I have to travel to Germany again for work. As soon as I arrived, Marie told me on the phone that a telegram with an invitation to a job interview arrived today. I should arrange an appointment. What a pleasant surprise, my first invitation to a job interview in Germany!

After the initial euphoria wears off, I need to come up with an idea of how to realize this interview as I am currently near Aschaffenburg and the company that invited me is based in Frankfurt/Main, thus not far from here.

I call there. Maybe I can get an appointment at short notice. Unfortunately, that is not possible and the earliest date would be next Monday at 10.30 a.m. I agree spontaneously but have to think about how to make this deadline. Since I will be in Germany until Friday for work purposes, the best solution would be if I stayed here for the weekend. To do so, I have to take one day's leave, which is approved by my company.

On Monday, November 21st, I am in Frankfurt/Main at 10.30 a.m. to attend the interview for the position of export clerk. I learned that a large number of candidates have applied for this position and ten applicants were invited to the first round of talks. Of these, only the top three would get a second appointment.

The interview goes well and once I am finished, a taxi takes me back to the nearby airport.

A quick phone call home brings another surprise. Today a letter arrived from Mainz with another invitation to a job interview. I should also contact this company by phone.

I call right away. Unfortunately, it is not possible to arrange a short-term appointment, the responsible department head is out of the office. Of course, that would have been too good to be true and thus I returned to the UK.

On Wednesday, November 23rd, another job-related trip to Germany is scheduled, this time to Offenbach. This is perfect because it might still be possible to arrange a meeting in Mainz.

I'm lucky. A job interview would be possible on Friday morning. This requires an additional leave day, which is also granted.

After my professional duties in Offenbach, a train takes me to Mainz on Thursday evening. Three weeks have passed since I specifically applied for real job offers. Now the second interview is coming up. Not bad.

The next morning, I arrived just in time. My interview partners show great interest in my international experience. My achievement is acknowledged, and this makes me proud. The advertised position is related to foreign marketing. Besides me, another candidate from Great Britain has applied. After the interview, I return to Frankfurt and a short while later I'm on the next flight to Birmingham.

On Sunday, November 27th, Rebecca is baptised at Melbourne Catholic Church.

We concluded that her godmother should be English, to offer Rebecca the possibility of a connection to the country where she was born. We asked Irene, and she immediately agreed which made us very happy.

We invite all our local friends to the christening. We will commemorate the event with our families during our next visit home. Since many of our friends are not Catholic, they are attending a christening ceremony of this denomination for the first time.

After the church service, we celebrate at home. We've prepared a buffet that everyone likes. Irene especially decorated the cake for her godchild with the flags of the three countries that Rebecca combines: Great Britain, France, and Germany. This was a very original idea. The cake not only looks beautiful, it also tastes delicious. The oldest couple in our circle of friends, Nancy and Wilfried, deserve the honour of a toast. Wilfried gives a wonderful speech for which we are very grateful.

That night, we go to bed tired but happy. All the guests liked our little party. Today was a beautiful day that we will fondly remember for a long time.

November passes, December begins, and with it comes a rejection from Frankfurt. This is a disappointment. But, you can't always win.

I continue to write applications and impatiently wait for an answer from Mainz. The days go by, and there is no answer.

On Friday, December 9th, the postman drops a letter into our mailbox. It's not the response I'm hoping for, but still good news. A company from the Stuttgart area invites me for an interview. I call them and arrange an appointment for Friday, December 16th.

Wednesday, December 14th is my last working day for 1988. The next day, I will be travelling to Stuttgart. When I get there, it is already dark. An employee of the company that invites me picks me up from the airport and takes me to a small town southwest of Stuttgart.

After I've settled into the hotel, there is time for a walk through the town. I somehow immediately feel very comfortable here on the edge of the Black Forest. This small town has a special flair. Our little daughter could grow up here safely. Back at the hotel, I sit down in the restaurant, order a delicious evening meal, and drink a refreshing beer.

The next morning, the HR manager picks me up from the hotel and drives me to the head office. During the morning, the two managing directors also occasionally participate in the conversation.

This company is looking for a new export manager. Naturally, there are many applicants for the position and the first interview usually lasts one to two hours. In my case, however, it is different today. Due to the distance between the company location and my current place of residence, both sides should use the time to find out as much as possible about each other. The HR manager even arranges a tour of the production facility.

In the evening, I leave the company with a positive feeling. I was able to obtain detailed information and am satisfied with the way the conversation went.

The HR manager drives me back to the airport. While driving, he informs me that there are usually at least two appointments before a decision is made. In my case, however, an exception will be made due to the distance and the associated travel costs. Both parties were able to get to know each other intensively today. Should the decision turn out in my favour, he would call me in Melbourne during the next week.

An hour later, I'm already on my way back home. During the landing approach at Heathrow airport, we fly over the brightly lit City of London. I recognise the House of Parliament, Buckingham Palace, and the brightly coloured Harrods department store. The pre-Christmas sea of lights of this cosmopolitan city is an unforgettable moment.

From London Heathrow, I continue to the East Midlands airport. When I get home around 9 p.m., I am confronted with less positive news. This morning, a letter of refusal arrived from Mainz. I had made it to second place with the company there, which is a remarkable achievement, but unfortunately received no job offer. Fortunately, this news did not reach me before the meeting in Stuttgart as my self-confidence would certainly have suffered a bit as a result. Naturally, I'm disappointed. However, thanks to today's job interview, my positive attitude quickly regained the upper hand. Now it's just a matter of being patient and waiting. A total of nine applications are currently in progress.

On Saturday, December 17th, my company's "Christmas Dinner Dance" takes place in the evening. As in previous years, this is a very happy event amongst colleagues. We eat and dance, and the mood is excellent. However, despite all the joy and festivities, I am in a pensive mood. Where will we celebrate Christmas next year?

The days go by, and I hope for a positive response from Stuttgart. Doubts arise over time. The ideal applicant for the position of export manager should have professional experience in sales, which I do not have. This came up during the job interview but didn't seem to be a problem. "The new job holder will be thoroughly trained", was the response given concerning this topic.

On Tuesday, December 20th, at around 5 p.m., I receive a phone call from my boss's secretary. She asked if I could interrupt my vacation for a day tomorrow to act as a translator during an important meeting with business partners in Frankfurt. I accept. The ticket will be deposited at the airport in Birmingham, where I can fetch it. I will meet my boss in Frankfurt, as he is currently in Sweden and will be travelling from there.

On Wednesday at 6 a.m., a taxi picks me up and takes me to the airport. At around 8.30 a.m. the plane to Frankfurt takes off. In the early stages of the flight, there are no special occurrences. We reach the coast, and the pilot warns of strong turbulence. The plane soon begins to vibrate slightly, then more violently. I'm used to that, it happens a few times on almost all flights. However, this time it gets worse and the fluctuations of the aircraft's movement increase in strength. Suddenly, the plane plunges. There is an enormous jerk. Fear spreads through the cabin. I don't like to fly with the older type of aircraft with which we are travelling at the moment. Only a few months ago, an aircraft of this type was said to have almost crashed due to engine problems. Not a big vote of confidence. The aircraft plunges down a second time, and this time the jerk is even harder. Some of the passengers become anxious, and sporadic screams can be heard. I start getting increasingly nervous too. During the next few minutes, we are shaken vigorously. I've never flown through such severe turbulence. Since we cannot climb any higher, the pilot pulls the plane down and the vibrations subside. Like all other passengers, I just want to get out of here. Luckily I'm booked on a more modern type of aircraft for the return flight.

Finally, we land in Frankfurt, I meet my boss, and a hire car takes us to our destination. The meeting is important and therefore takes longer than planned. Instead of 4.40 p.m. as scheduled, we fly back at 6 p.m. That wouldn't matter if it weren't for us having to board the same older type of aircraft as this morning. I can only hope that there will be no more turbulence.

However, the return flight was smooth, and I was relieved.

The week is almost over, and the answer from Stuttgart is still pending.

I've been applying for a job in Germany for three months now. So far, without success.

Thursday, December 22nd. Today is the last day before we leave for France. The HR manager, whose call I'm waiting for, knows this. Thus, he would have to call during the day.

The excitement increases. Should we receive a positive answer, this would once again fundamentally change our lives.

The morning passes, and the phone remains silent.

At noon it rings. I pick up the phone, curious, hoping that the person I'm expecting is at the other end of the line. He is. Then, everything happens very quickly. The company has decided to offer me the job. Should I still be interested in the advertised position of export manager, the employment contract will be sent to me. I confirm my interest. As soon as I've received the contract, I shall terminate my current employment with one month's notice. The start of the new job would be February 1, 1989.

I hang up the phone and still cannot believe my luck. It's true! It is really true! They have chosen me. I will receive an employment contract. We are overjoyed. Our little daughter is probably the only person in the house who is not aware of this important moment. She is still far too young to understand that at this moment our life has once again taken a very specific direction.

In the afternoon, I take a stroll through Melbourne with Rebecca in the baby-carrying strap. The initial joy about my success has faded, and something like the melancholy of farewell arises. Now it is certain. In just a few weeks, we shall be leaving this village, this region, and this country. We lived in the UK for four years. During this time, Derbyshire became our second home. Now we're going to leave all of this again. However, we decided to return to Germany ourselves, nobody forced us to do this.

It's a grey, windy afternoon, and Rebecca is sleeping in the carrying strap. I walk down to the pond. During the summer we often came here, sat on a bench, enjoyed the tranquillity of this place, and watched the ducks. Then I directed my steps to the small village clinic, where we took part in a pregnancy course together with other expectant parents. During the walk, I remembered all the good times we spent in Melbourne. Although I'm looking forward to the new challenge, saying goodbye to the familiar surroundings is harder than expected.

On Friday, December 23rd, we travel to Paris. A colleague and his wife, who is also French, accompany us. They want to spend Christmas with their families like we do.

In France, we inform our family about the upcoming changes in our lives. They are all very happy because it will be much easier for them to visit us in Germany than in Britain. Especially now that we have a child, they want to see their granddaughter more often. We toast the news. The champagne corks pop, we chink glasses. To a successful future.

I am only staying in France over the Christmas holidays because I have to go back to work on January 3rd. I am also awaiting the new employment contract. Once it is signed, I have to give notice to my current employer so that I can start my new job on February 1st. Marie and Rebecca will return on January 6th.

Irene and John invited me for New Year's Eve. This will be my last year-end in the UK. Friends and neighbours also attend the party. It's a lovely evening with a cold buffet, cakes, and Irene's wonderful homemade filled chocolates.

I keep the news about my job-related change to myself until just after midnight. Only when all the other guests have left do I inform Irene and John about the upcoming change. They are simultaneously very surprised while also being happy for us and regretting that we shall soon be so far away from them. Then it will no longer be possible to drop by for a cup of tea at short notice.

On Sunday, January 1, 1989, I want to say goodbye to the land-scape that was my home during the last four years. I drive to Blackbrook, take a look at our former house where we were so happy during the summer of 1987, walk along the footpath behind the garden, admire the landscape, and find it hard to suppress a growing melancholy.

My next destination is Matlock Bath. We often came here on Sunday afternoons, took a stroll along the main street, looked at the shop windows, and enjoyed a cup of tea. Those were relaxing moments. I will always remember them.

I drive on, stop at an inn for a meal, visit Chatsworth House, and continue via Bakewell to Buxton. Along the way, I passed places where we spent carefree hours with friends. There is an antique market in Buxton this afternoon.

On the way back, I stop by Nancy and Wilfried on Mount Pleasant in Belper. For the childless couple, we were like their own children during the last few years. I think it was above all the friendship and warmth of all the people we were able to count among our closest circle of friends in Britain that were decisive in making us feel at home here and why we seldom suffered from homesickness. Nancy and Wilfried's door was also always open to us, like that of a parent's house. Like Irene and John, they are happy about our success but also sad that we shall soon be leaving.

On Monday, January 2nd, I start packing. The employment contract from Germany has arrived. I sign it, send it back, and give notice to my current employer. My boss understands and respects my decision and wishes me all the best. He would have liked to keep me but cannot offer me a higher position in the near future.

During the last three years, I have been able to gain valuable experience, for which I am very grateful. There have been ups and downs, days of success but also days of frustration. Nevertheless, this time will always remain part of my work experience. I can only hope that the decision to change jobs was the right one and that I will find the task I envision in the new company.

Changing jobs is always risky. The decision to move to another country was also risky. Now that we know how well it all went, we're glad we took that risk. Why shouldn't the return to one's own country be just as successful? We are in good spirits and not afraid.

On Friday, January 6th, Marie and Rebecca returned from France. I pick them up from Birmingham airport. From a distance, I can see the aircraft's powerful headlights in the dark sky. After the landing I relaxed, everything went well, and my two ladies returned safely. I'm looking forward to seeing them again. One week is quite a long time, and Rebecca has changed again.

During the next few weeks, we pack all our belongings. Time goes by quickly, and there is a lot to do. Every evening after work, I spend a few hours packing. We stow the entire household contents in crates and boxes, disassemble furniture, and store everything in the large double garage. All items can be set up there in such a way that they can quickly and easily be loaded onto the furniture lorry.

As we once again cross national borders, all boxes and cartons must be accurately numbered and a detailed list of their contents has to be generated.

I ask my boss for a job reference. As with previous British employers, he is also surprised about this request. It seems unusual to get a written job reference in this country and it is more common that the new employer calls the previous one to receive information. However, since it is different in my country, he did me the favour of writing me a very good reference. I shouldn't have any problems applying for jobs in the future.

I will officially start my new job on February 1st. However, my new employer asked if I could be present at a trade fair in Cologne during the last week of January to meet important foreign customers. I talk to my boss about the possibility of an early leave, and he approves it.

One evening, the phone rings. At the other end of the line, the colleague whose house we are currently renting would like to discuss our move out of the house. We are planning to leave at the end of January and he naturally would like to have a new tenant for the remaining months until his return. Conveniently, another colleague is currently looking for a temporary rental property and I set up the contact, and soon both parties agree on the terms and conditions. Hence, this issue has been solved to everyone's satisfaction.

Now it's getting serious. Our belongings are packed, and a transport company from Derby will collect them on January 24th, drive them to the south coast, and take them to the ferry. On the other side of the English Channel, the freight is taken over by a German transport company and taken on to the final destination. Since we currently do not have any accommodation at the new location yet, our belongings will initially be stored there with a local forwarding company.

Now it's time to say goodbye. On Saturday, January 21st, we invite Irene and John for dinner at a restaurant in Derby. It is a very pleasant evening.

Marie and Rebecca can stay with them for almost two weeks after my departure until they follow on Friday, February 3rd.

On Sunday, January 22nd, we say goodbye to Nancy and Wilfried. They invited us to their house for dinner. As always, Nancy cooked very well. As a starter, we eat half a melon with sherry, as main course an excellent steak with vegetables, and for dessert, there is ice cream and trifle. Nancy's trifle is as good as Irene's filled chocolates.

Every farewell is difficult and hurts. But we comfort ourselves with the fact that we shall see each other again soon. All our friends can visit us and we can come back here to visit them.

On Monday, January 23rd, we finished packing. All crates and boxes are numbered, and the contents are carefully listed. Rebecca is now six months old, and she seems to sense our tension and is restless.

On Tuesday, the furniture lorry arrives at 10 a.m. Everything is loaded, the lorry departs, and all our belongings are now on their way.

I drive to the office, today is my last day at work. Tomorrow I will fly to Frankfurt together with my boss for a last meeting where I translate for him. After that, my employment with this company will end and I will take the train from Frankfurt to the trade fair in Cologne to start working for my new employer.

In the office, I say goodbye to all of my colleagues, addresses are exchanged, and one promises to write to one another, perhaps to visit one day, and in any case to keep in touch. I receive many gifts, very nice souvenirs from the Derby area, including a book about Derbyshire, bone china from neighbouring Staffordshire, and a wonderful lace tablecloth from Nottingham.

On Wednesday, a colleague picks me up at 6 a.m. and drives me to the airport in Birmingham. I get into the car, fasten the seat belt, and take one last look at the house where we lived for a year and where Rebecca spent the first six months of her life. Then we leave the residential area, cross through Melbourne, whose residents are still asleep, and shortly afterwards are on the main road to Birmingham.

Daylight is slowly breaking and I am travelling down this road for the last time on which I so often drove during the last three years to pick up customers or business partners from the airport or drive them back. There is always a first and a last time. This is now the last time.

The plane to Frankfurt is on time. We slowly approach the

runway, the pilot gives thrust, the jet engines accelerate, and then we take off. At this very moment, I am leaving Great Britain. This country, which is now slowly disappearing beneath me, was also my home for four years. Our first daughter was born here, we made friends.

When will I come back? What awaits me in the future?

I look out the window, down at the countryside, the meadows and pastures bordered by hedges, the trees, streets and houses. Now that I'm leaving this country, I feel homesick. A few months ago, I thought it would be easy to leave and start something new, but now I realize it won't be that easy. Right now, it is very difficult to give this all up. I calm myself with the thought of coming back here as often as I can, to visit friends, to walk in Derbyshire, and just to be here again.

The landscape below me disappears in the haze of the clouds that we are now flying through and a deep blue sky awaits us above the clouds. "Goodbye, Great Britain", it has been a very special time, and I shall never forget it.

RETURNING FROM GREAT BRITAIN TO GERMANY

The flight takes around ninety minutes. The aircraft brings me back from our adopted home of the last four years to my own native country. We land in Frankfurt, drive to our destination, conduct a successful meeting, and return to the airport. There, it is finally time to say goodbye to my boss and the colleague who also attended today's meeting. While they return to the UK, I take the train to Cologne. We shake hands, they wish me well, and take the escalator to the terminal. I watch them until they're out of sight.

This moment is truly the conclusion of my four-year adventure in the UK, which began on March 11, 1985, when I landed in Harwich and ends today on January 25, 1989, at Frankfurt airport.

Technically, the story would end here. I have taken you, the reader, with me on a journey in which you were able to experience how I left Germany to seek my fortune in Great Britain, how I found work, enhanced my career prospects, and managed to return to Germany.

However, the return to my native country turned out to be anything but easy. To also share this difficult process with you, I will continue to report on the events of 1989, the year in which we tried to return to Germany after four successful years in the UK.

After my two British colleagues disappeared down the escalator, I entered the train station at Frankfurt airport. An express train takes me from there to Cologne, and a taxi drops me off at my hotel. That evening, I go to bed early because firstly, I am very tired, and secondly I want to be fit and rested tomorrow.

At breakfast, I meet my first new colleagues, with whom I drive to the exhibition centre. The booth of my future employer is impressive! The trade fair has been running for a few days. Today is my first day, and my colleagues have been working at the booth since the trade fair opened.

Naturally, I know almost no one in this company. In the crowd, I spot the sales manager I met during the interview. He will be my new boss. I greet him. He gives me a friendly welcome but seems to be in a hurry and asks me to support the export secretary. During the interview in December, I also briefly got to know the secretary of the export department, and I set out to find her.

My new employer is a medium-sized family business. I also met the company owner during the interview. He is also present and greets me, but has little time.

I keep looking for the export secretary, find her, and offer my support. She doesn't usually attend fairs. However, since the previous export manager had only recently left the company, she stepped in.

I imagined my first day in the new company to be a bit different. After all, during the interview, there was great interest in my university degree and several years of work experience in Britain. Therefore, I assumed that as a new employee, I would be officially introduced to the staff and business partners on the first day. However, nothing of the sort happens.

The main reason why they wanted me to attend the trade fair one week before the official start of work was so that I get to know the most important foreign customers and business partners. Now, I am amazed to discover that the daughter of the company owner looks after precisely this group of people and translates if necessary. I learned that she studied business economics and speaks several foreign languages.

I will use the next few days to introduce myself, to actively support my colleagues, to get to know the new products and, especially, to make a good impression.

On Saturday evening, the management invites all employees present at the booth to dinner. The CEO gives a speech and also compliments the performance of the export secretary, who stepped in at short notice to support the department. I am not mentioned at all. It would have been a good opportunity to introduce me as a new employee. Why doesn't he do this? I can't think of a suitable answer at the moment.

Just a few weeks ago, I was informed that I had been chosen from several qualified applicants. I've been at the booth for four days, was hardly noticed, and above all not officially introduced. There is something wrong!

I travel to the small town on the edge of the Black Forest where my new employer is based on Sunday evening. When I get there around 9 p.m., I feel unwell. Did I catch a cold? How quickly one can catch a virus in a crowded exhibition hall.

At the hotel, I immediately take a hot shower and go to bed. Soon, I start sweating profusely. Hopefully, it is nothing serious as it wouldn't be a good start to this new phase of my life.

The next morning, I don't feel very well but don't want to start my first day in the head office with a sick note. I go to the office and find out that the export secretary is absent, she is on sick leave.

In the course of the morning, I receive a detailed on-the-job training plan for the next two months from the HR department. It shows that I will pass through all departments. The HR manager assures me that I will be trained thoroughly. My predecessor was older than me. This time, however, the company preferred to recruit a younger candidate as they intend to thoroughly train and develop their new employee. The training plan seems to confirm this.

During the first week of February, I start looking for accommodation. I was told that it won't be easy to find something suitable in this area and the sooner I start searching, the better.

First of all, I have to find temporary accommodation that is also suitable for a small family. Since I don't have a vehicle yet, I'm allowed to use a company car in the evening to drive around. Some hotels and guesthouses would also offer rooms for a longer period, but these are very small with no cooking facilities.

A colleague gave me the tip to look for a holiday flat. I do this, look at one, and can even rent it at a reasonable price for the next few weeks. It has four rooms, a kitchen, and bathroom, is fully furnished, and even a cot is available. The first hurdle has been passed.

On Friday, February 3rd, I fetch Marie and Rebecca from Stuttgart airport. Luckily I can use a company car. Rebecca is now six months old and I don't want to miss one more day of her development. She was the main reason why we wanted to move as quickly as possible. Tonight the three of us are reunited. For the time being, we have a temporary flat, and now we just have to find a long-term accommodation.

However, this is becoming increasingly difficult. Regardless of who I ask, the answers are anything but encouraging.

Unfortunately, there are only a few adverts in the newspaper but I do discover some interesting rental offers and want to view the rental properties on Saturday. Naturally, we are not the only interested parties, especially given the limited number of offers.

We look at two rental properties and leave our name and address as the owners say they will call us. However, due to the high demand, I am not very optimistic. We cannot achieve more on this day.

I keep searching. There must be other ways to get addresses. During the next few days, I call some real estate agents, municipal administrations, newspapers, and the real estate departments of local savings banks. There must be suitable accommodation for us somewhere in this area.

The HR manager informs me about a house that is for rent. It is still under construction but should be ready for occupancy in a month or two. I immediately contact the landlord and he tells me that there are already many interested parties.

I am familiarising myself with the new job, getting to know the products and organisational structure, and adapting to the new working environment. However, this does not always run as smoothly as one would like. Intrigue, prejudice, and envy play a bigger role than one thinks. However, at least the on-the-job training is extremely professional.

Regarding accommodation, I call everywhere and am finally successful.

The first lead is at a savings bank in the neighbouring town. A new block of flats is being built, in which there is still one flat to let. I received the caretaker's name and phone number and called him. The information is confirmed, a three-room flat is still available. I make an appointment to view it.

The second lead is at the real estate department of a local bank. They know about a terraced house to let. The owner, a customer of the bank, only informed them this morning that he wanted to rent out the house. How fortunate that I'm calling right now! The property is practically not on the market yet, and thus no one but me knows about it. I get the landlord's name and telephone number, call him, and arrange an appointment to view the house.

What a liberating feeling to finally be successful.

The next day, we looked at the three-room flat. It is spacious but has the disadvantage that it is still under construction and will only be ready for occupancy in about three to four months. The rent without additional costs would be 780 D-Mark per month. The caretaker notes our name and telephone number.

On Friday evening, we visit the terraced house. The rent is around 1,100 D-Mark per month, which is a lot more expensive than the flat. However, we would also get much more for that price. The house has four rooms, a garden, and a garage. Although the rent is at the upper end of what we can afford, it would be manageable. We could move in on April 1st, which would naturally be very convenient for us. In five weeks we would already have our own home again. In addition, we would not have to pay a broker's commission, because the landlord's bank does not charge a commission. This is a great advantage because real estate agents in this area charge up to 2.5 months' rent. The garden would be ideal for our little daughter, and even though the house is on the outskirts in a quiet residential area the city centre can be reached within a few minutes on foot. The landlord is friendly and makes a good impression on us, and he evidently likes us too. If we want to rent the house, we have to make a quick decision as once it hits the market, other interested parties will surely show up. We are currently the first and only ones to know about this rental property and immediately fall in love with this house. It is expensive but would make a nice and safe home. We decide quickly and agree with the landlord to sign the rental contract next week.

That evening we were very happy. We found a house with a garden and confidence returned. Things hadn't been so good lately. Although we always thought it would be easy to return to Germany we now had to realize that after four years in the UK, we've put down deeper roots than previously thought. We have also changed, adopted different practices and ways of thinking, and accepted a different system. We now have to get used to another currency, right-hand traffic, and somehow also to a different mentality.

We constantly think about the UK, feel increasingly homesick, and miss our friends, and didn't expect such strong feelings after returning. Luckily we have our little daughter. She is now almost seven months old and developing splendidly. Moreover, the fact that we will soon be able to live in a new home again makes us more confident about our situation.

Since I started working for the company, I have neither had a meeting with my boss nor did I receive any information from him. So far, I've only met him on two occasions, during the interview and at the booth. The reason for this is probably due to the training period.

However, internal information from colleagues makes me think. The daughter of the company owner will soon join the company. Which field of responsibility will she be interested in? Management? Marketing? Foreign markets?

In mid-February, I accompany the other export manager through the Netherlands to visit customers. This is a very good opportunity for me to get to know his area of responsibility as well as the new products, to take part in sales talks, and to get to know the sales policy and other important details.

Back in the office, the HR manager explained to me that while I would be making an important career move as an export manager this also involves risks and dangers that I have to be aware of.

On Friday evening, February 24th, I sign the tenancy agreement for the terraced house. It has a term of three years and can be extended thereafter. We really did it! Despite the tense situation in the housing market, we were able to find a nice home after only four weeks of intensive searching and didn't even have to pay a broker's fee. In five weeks, we will finally have our own home again.

Our success story also seems to be continuing in Germany.

FAILURE IN GERMANY

When you risk a lot, you can also lose a lot. Currently, we are still on the road to success.

A new week begins, the sixth for me in this company. According to the on-the-job training, I am in the purchasing department today. The supervisor guides me through the raw materials warehouse, explains its structure, and shows me various materials.

On Tuesday, February 28th, I am in the purchasing department again. A colleague is just explaining various material groups to me when the phone rings. The call is for me, the sales manager wants to see me. Finally, there seems to be the first opportunity for a personal conversation.

I have to wait a moment in the antechamber, then my new boss invites me to take a seat at the conference table in his office. We sit across from each other, and he avoids direct eye contact. I immediately sense that something is wrong.

He gets straight to the point. Since I do not have sufficient experience in the export business, he considers further training to be too time-consuming. He requires someone who could immediately fill the position of export manager.

I'm completely shocked and taken aback! This man now claims exactly the opposite of what was clarified during the interview and what the HR manager had always emphasised. Until now, it was always said that this time a conscious decision was made in favour of a young and therefore still relatively inexperienced applicant, who should be trained thoroughly. Now, it seems that management would like to have an experienced person. Why this sudden change of mind? It cannot be due to a lack of interest or commitment on my part.

I want to know a plausible reason for this serious change of opinion. Why should I suddenly no longer be suitable for this position when I haven't even been able to prove it? He evades my questions and doesn't give a reason. How can this man assess someone he doesn't even really know?

I keep trying to find a comprehensible reason for this sudden change of mind. However, either he does not want to comment on this, or there is no reason. He just keeps highlighting the lack of experience. Since my probationary period is not yet over, the company can terminate my employment without giving reasons with a notice period of one month.

The conversation lasted around ten minutes, and he then called in the HR manager. All formalities are to be clarified with him.

The HR manager doesn't talk much, and we go to his office. Once we are seated, he informs me that he was only notified about this decision yesterday. I am not sure whether I should believe him. After all, he is the head of the HR department of this company and should have a say in such drastic decisions.

He doesn't have time to talk to me at length at the moment either. We make an appointment for 2 p.m.

I try to stay calm and to think analytically. There must be a solution that is acceptable to both sides. Maybe I can at least get details from the HR manager. If I want to defend myself, I need facts.

I return to the department where I'm scheduled to be trained today. Actually, I should spend the whole day there, but due to the new situation only stay until noon and then return to my desk.

This all comes as a complete surprise, and I have absolutely no idea how to proceed. Professionally, I've already coped with quite a few challenges in areas where I had no experience. I had always faced the respective challenges, mastered them, and gained valuable skills and know-how in the process. Therefore, I am convinced that with the necessary support, I could also be successful in this company. However, it seems that they don't want to provide this support here.

I reflect on the situation. During my application phase, other companies in this area also showed interest in my career. After signing the current employment contract, I didn't pursue these offers any further. That, I now realize, was a mistake. Luckily I have not yet cancelled the appointments with these companies. Maybe it's not too late. I should take every chance now.

In addition, the headquarters of a company that manufactures coordinate measuring machines is not far away from my current location. As I know the product and the market from my work in Britain, I should definitely visit this particular company.

It's now 2 p.m., time to meet the HR manager again. In his office, I made another attempt to find out the exact reason why I was offered an employment contract just a few months ago that they are now unwilling to comply with. The HR manager evades my question and states that he doesn't know the reason.

Maybe, he adds, I should have been visiting clients right away instead of being trained. Now this is amazing! It was he himself who put together my detailed training plan. And if that were the case, why has no one commented on this yet? Until today, the sales manager hasn't even spoken to me. So far, it has always been said that I will be trained thoroughly on the job. Even though the HR manager understands perfectly well that I want to know a plausible reason he cannot provide one. Incredible!

Actually, I should be glad that I don't have to work here any longer. Despite all the tragedy, I feel something like relief. I didn't feel comfortable in this company from the first day anyway.

Finally, I would like to know the position that the daughter of the company owner is aiming for when she joins the company in the near future. My counterpart notices what I'm up to. He doesn't think she's aiming for the position of the export manager but he can't rule that out either.

We now discuss the formalities. I will be released with immediate effect, my salary will be paid for another month, and I can also keep the company car for that long. At least that keeps me mobile. Half of the removal expenses will be reimbursed. As far as the tenancy agreement for the terraced house is concerned, the company is trying to find a new tenant internally.

I return to my desk, pack up and leave the office. At the door, I stop and turn around. However, there's no point in looking back. There is only the past. I should rather look ahead because that's where I can react.

I close the door and am very disappointed. Two months ago, the return to my country seemed to be successful. Now, I've lost everything. What lies ahead for us? No one asked about my wife or our seven-month-old daughter. No one showed the slightest interest in how they were doing. We have been living in a holiday flat for three weeks and were so excited to move into the terraced house. That's all over now!

There is still a hard road ahead of me. How will Marie react if I tell her what has happened? Since we've been through so much already I am sure she'll be very disappointed but still composed.

I get into the car, drive home, and inform my wife. For her, it is also a huge shock as neither of us expected such a development. It completely changes the direction our life seemed to be taking until today. If yesterday we thought that we could spend the coming years in this area, today we don't know how everything will continue.

That evening, I walk through the small village in which our holiday flat is located and think about the current situation. It is already dark and starting to drizzle. Could I proceed in the same way in my own country as in Britain? Perhaps I could also achieve something quickly by being proactive. I should visit some local companies during the next few days and spontaneously introduce myself. Above all, I should especially contact those companies that had shown an interest in getting to know me just a few weeks ago.

The walk is good for me. I gather new strength, and courage, and gain confidence. After all, it is best not to rely on others, but only on oneself. At home, Marie has also recovered from the initial shock. Rebecca is sleeping, we sit down in the living room and have time to talk. I explain my plan. Tomorrow, I will visit one of the companies in Stuttgart that had contacted me in Britain and had shown an interest in my previous career.

We have hope again. Maybe everything will go faster than expected.

In the middle of the night, I wake up to a feeling of fear, which is intensified by the darkness and total silence. The job is gone, our home in Britain as well, the future is uncertain, and our friends are far away. Where shall we go? Where shall we live? How quickly can I find a new job? I lie awake and can't go back to sleep.

That night, I hit the absolute low point of my life. I took a great risk and lost. If we were at the very top on Friday evening after signing the tenancy agreement, now, just a few days later, we're at the very bottom.

Why did I trust so blindly? If we had kept the house in

Melbourne a little longer, a return would have been possible. I had also applied to an international company in the East Midlands which expressed interest. But that's far away now. We wanted to embrace the new life too quickly, lost, and now have to deal with the consequences.

I try to go back to sleep but it's difficult. Too many thoughts are running through my head.

Wednesday, March 1st. Bright sunshine in the morning. I drive to Stuttgart, reach the company that I intend to visit today, get past the porter without any problems thanks to the reply letter I received at the time, and a few minutes later I'm in the personnel office.

The HR manager is surprised to learn what has happened to me in the meantime and advises me to remain confident. He does not understand such a practice. This one misfortune, he assures me, will not spoil my CV. With four years of international experience in Britain, I have good chances in the job market. The conversation does me good. Now it would be ideal if there was a current vacancy for which I could be considered. Unfortunately, there are no specific vacancies, but in the near future, the position of a country manager and an export clerk should be filled. Based on my previous career, he wants to find out whether I would be suitable for one of the two positions.

I applied to this company at random a few months ago and there was no real job offer. Now, however, my situation has changed. I can't wait a few weeks or even months for a vacancy to be filled, I need a job now, at least during the next three to four weeks. The HR manager understands that, picks up the phone, and calls the head of the department looking for an export clerk. Although they preferred a much younger applicant, he agreed to conduct an interview. It takes a good hour, and doesn't lead to success due to my age, but gives me a lot of self-confidence. The head of the department looking for a country manager is currently on vacation. Unfortunately, I can't talk to him today. This position would suit me, says the HR manager. But first I have to talk to the person in charge. I should call next week to arrange an appointment.

After this conversation, I spontaneously decided to visit a company that manufactures coordinate measuring machines. Their head office is just an hour's drive away from Stuttgart. I'm quite confident. However, this confidence ends abruptly at the factory gate. Without a letter of invitation, I cannot get through. As I had not contacted this company in the past I do not have such a letter. At least I can call HR from the gatehouse, albeit without any success. I have to apply in writing. The journey was in vain.

On the way back, my mood drops. The euphoria of this morning is gone. It won't be as easy in Germany as it was in Britain.

In the evening, I call my parents. I wanted to avoid this conversation - who likes to talk about defeat after all? But looking for a job will take some time, and we cannot stay in the holiday flat that long. There is space in my parents' house, and we could also store the furniture there.

They are surprised but react very well. There is no problem staying with them for a while. We make plans to visit them next weekend to discuss everything.

Thursday, March 2nd. In the morning, I ring up two companies that I've previously contacted. I can visit one of them today, and the other one next Monday.

The job interview in the afternoon goes very well. I talk to the chief marketing officer (CMO) as the general manager is on vacation. The CMO is primarily interested in my international experience. I should call in a week or two to arrange an appointment with the general manager.

After this conversation, I have a positive feeling. I appeared self-confident, the negative experience did not burden me. This positive mood makes me dare an experiment on the way home. I would like to find out whether it is also possible in Germany, just like in Britain, to simply knock on company doors and ask for a job.

I spot a medium-sized company, stop, and ask at the gate if I may speak to HR. To my surprise, I am not turned away but am told to wait for a moment. After a few minutes, an elderly gentleman appears. I immediately notice that he does not understand what I want. I explained it to him, described my situation, and asked for a job. We speak English, then he switches to French. At the end of the conversation, it turns out that the company owner himself is standing in front of me. Unfortunately, he currently has no vacancies in the domain for which I could be considered. Nevertheless, this spontaneous conversation at the factory gate was a partial success. I wasn't turned away and was able to have an instant conversation with the company owner.

I'm starting to enjoy the experiment. On the rest of the way home, I stop at eight other companies that I find interesting in terms of their size and appearance. However, this approach is unfortunately unsuccessful and I am told that I have to apply in writing first as this is the way things are done in Germany. However, whether it is also the most effective approach remains to be seen.

In the evening, the positive feeling prevails, as the experience I bring from my previous career is still met with great interest.

Friday, March 3rd. Today I have another appointment with the HR manager of my current employer. There are still some formalities to be clarified.

To be sure that I left nothing unchecked, I invested 50 D-Mark in a lawyer to find out whether I could assert claims due to financial disadvantages. I am told that this is not the case. During the probation period, employment can be terminated by either party without giving reasons. As far as the tenancy agreement for the house is concerned, these are "private investment costs" and are solely my risk. That's what happens when you take too many risks. I learned this lesson. It won't happen to me again next time.

That evening, I will have to inform the owner of the house we intend to rent that we will be cancelling the agreement. He doesn't know anything yet. How will he react?

He reacts reasonably, understands the situation, and wants to help. With the current situation in the housing market, it shouldn't be too difficult to find a new tenant soon. However, if this is not possible by the first of the month, a monthly rent has to be paid.

We visit my parents over the weekend and discuss how to proceed. Two rooms on the attic floor are available, and our furniture can be stored in the basement. During this visit, I also intend to buy a small second-hand car, and am lucky and find one that I can currently afford.

Monday, March 6th. Today I have an appointment with a company near Heilbronn. I applied to this company in November and was invited to an interview but was unable to attend the appointment. However, this job interview does not lead to success because the advertised post requires special experience. It is good that such important criteria are already clarified during the interview so that there are no surprises afterwards.

During the week, I visit some companies around Stuttgart, take part in an interview with a management consultancy, and spontaneously try to get in contact with HR managers. I am not always successful but achieve some promising results like talking to the owner of a small machine tool factory. He is currently looking for an employee in purchasing. Should I be interested, I could apply. However, I am more interested in sales. At least I managed to get through to the company owner and had an interesting conversation without an appointment. Sometimes this approach seems to work, even in Germany.

I also called the company that I had a first meeting with last week when the head of the department was on vacation. Now he's back, and I get an appointment for Friday.

This interview is very interesting. However, the position of country manager will not be available until June at the earliest and I'll have to wait. However, waiting is only good if you have a job but I cannot afford to wait. I have to get back to work as soon as possible. Hence, I don't have high hopes, as it will certainly take too long.

On Saturday, March 18th, we left our temporary home which has not brought us any luck. We are proud to have kept calm and acted prudently. All in all, our retreat is well-regulated. Our furniture will follow on Monday. A truck will transport it from Baden-Wuerttemberg to Bavaria. When we packed and loaded the furniture two months ago, we never thought it would take so long to finally get it back.

In my parents' house, the boxes and furniture are stored in the basement, and we move into the two rooms on the attic floor.

One of them becomes the children's room, and the other one our combined living and bedroom.

This week, I also signed the cancellation of the tenancy agreement. The owner of the house found a new tenant for the 1st of May and thus we only have to pay rent for one month but after that, we are released from our contractual obligations. We are satisfied with this arrangement, as it could have been worse.

I apply to job adverts every week now. When I still had a job, I didn't care about the time. Now, without a job, waiting is difficult but I have to be patient.

On Wednesday, March 29th, I handed in the company car as agreed and returned home by train. As the train leaves the station, I take one last look at the surrounding landscape. On the other side of the valley, at the edge of the forest, I recognise for a brief moment the terraced house that should have become our new home in a few days. Now everything has turned out completely different, and another family will move in there. Hopefully, we will soon find a new home as well.

On Tuesday, April 4th, I've been invited for an interview with the CEO of the company where I've already had the opportunity to talk to the CMO. I leave early, as it is a long journey to get there.

The interview lasts one hour. This company is looking for an employee who especially focuses on the British market. After the on-site training, the suitable candidate should develop sales in Britain. Until now, this company had never really managed to gain a foothold in the UK market. This sounds very tempting as it would involve a return to Britain. If my family were still in Melbourne, that could have been a really interesting offer. However, we decided, mainly because of our child, to return to the Continent and thus it is now too late to move back to the UK.

I keep applying for jobs. April goes by, and there are no invitations for interviews. If I cannot visit a sufficient number of companies directly in Germany, wouldn't it make more sense to search abroad again? I could apply to domestic companies in writing, but in the meantime also become active abroad. The time would thus be used efficiently and my morale would get a huge boost.

A plan begins to mature. Which country would be suitable? I've been to the UK and improved my knowledge of the English language, and thus I should now focus on a country with a different language. What could be better than my wife's native country, France?

I start developing a plan. What a liberating feeling to become active. All of this is still just a vague concept. So far, I haven't seen any chance of finding a qualified job in France because my proficiency in French is not nearly as good as in English.

PROACTIVE JOB SEARCH IN FRANCE AND GERMANY

Since I have a plan, I feel liberated. I should leave and actively determine my future path in life. There is a city in the French Alps that I have been interested in for a while, Grenoble. I focus my planning on this place. Just like in Britain in 1985, I could offer my language skills, special knowledge, and professional experience to local companies there. I have nothing to lose. With a bit of luck, I could succeed.

The plan becomes more precise. I am highly motivated but keep it to myself for the time being, translate my CV into French, and explore a travel route through Switzerland.

Thursday, April 20th. The phone rings in the afternoon. A company from Munich invites me for an interview on Wednesday next week, thereby halting the Grenoble project for the time being. Shortly afterwards, I receive another invitation to Frankfurt. That means there are two job interviews for next week.

The meeting in Munich is postponed at short notice, and thus the only date that remains is the interview in Frankfurt. However, the position to be filled does not require any foreign language skills and I didn't invest four years in the English language to not use this skill in a professional context.

On Saturday morning, April 29th, I set out to realize the plan, which until now has only existed in theory. Camping equipment plus provisions are in the car, and copies of certificates and my

CV in French are ready to hand. I feel completely free, take my destiny back into my own hands, and act instead of waiting. I'm not afraid, as I already have experience in searching for employment in a foreign country. What I was able to achieve in the UK may also be feasible in France.

Today's route should get me as far as Lake Geneva.

At Lindau, I cross the Austrian border, pass Bregenz and shortly afterwards I'm in Switzerland. The landscape is magnificent, and the mountains radiate peace and security. Originally I intended to drive along the edge of the Alps. However, due to the beauty of the landscape, I spontaneously changed my route, drove to Chur, and intended to cross over two alpine passes to reach the Rhone Valley and to continue through the Valais to Montreux. Unfortunately, this is not possible. Signs indicate that the roads over the Oberalp and Furka passes are still closed. I could have imagined that. At the end of April, most of the alpine passes are still closed. Hence, there is no point in driving up the Upper Rhine Valley, as there will be no getting through further up.

I turn around and choose a different route. It is now afternoon and I realize that I won't be able to reach Montreux today and I thus change today's final destination to Lucerne.

It's already starting to get dark when I arrive there, find the campsite without any problems, and pitch my tent. Afterwards, I stroll along the lake shore. In front of me, Lake Lucerne lies dreamily in the sunset, the peaks of snow-covered giants are shining in the distance, and the first lights of the city are flashing across from the other bank. It is pleasantly quiet. I pass magnificent hotels, behind whose windows guests are seated at finely set tables. I feel free, take a deep breath, and am on my way to a new adventure.

Sunday, April 30th. The morning is filled with bright sunshine and I disassemble the tent and travel on. While Lucerne was familiar to me, Grenoble is completely unknown.

Past Bern, I cross the so-called Röstigraben near Fribourg, marking the language border between German- and French-speaking Switzerland.

Around noon, I reach Lake Geneva, stop briefly at a picnic area high above Lausanne, and enjoy the fantastic view over the city and the surrounding landscape. France is already visible on the other side of the lake. Somewhere behind the mountains lies Grenoble, the destination of my journey. However, there is still a long way to go.

After Geneva, I cross the French border, pass Annecy and Chambery, and reach my destination at around 4 p.m. There it is in front of me, the city of Grenoble in France, like Derby in Great Britain four years ago. Maybe it will become our new home, who knows? That mainly depends on how successful my job search will be.

I buy a street map at a petrol station, look for a campsite, and quickly find what I'm looking for. However, the site does not look particularly inviting. Therefore I drove on and discovered a nicer site, which unfortunately is still closed.

It's getting late now, and if I still want to pitch the tent during daylight, something suitable should be found quickly. Hence I return to Grenoble only to find that the local campsite is now fully occupied. In Voiron, a small village not far from here, there is another option for campers. I make my way there immediately, am lucky, the site is open and there are still enough free pitches.

Monday, May 1st. The first day of May is also a public holiday in France and I thus cannot visit any companies today but use the time for preliminary explorations. The locations of all major companies are provided on the street map. I plan to go there to get a first impression, and after working out a route, I set off.

Some of the companies are familiar to me, such as a large PC and printer manufacturer and a maker of construction machinery. The other companies are completely unfamiliar to me.

I approach six companies in three industrial estates. The PC and printer manufacturer seems to be the most interesting, the facility is brand new. Contented, I return to the campsite and relax in the evening sun.

Tuesday, May 2nd. Today, things are getting serious. At 8 a.m., I shower, the sanitary facilities are perfect. To make a good impression in the event of any job interviews, I put on trendy trousers, a smart shirt, a tie, and the right jacket. Hence, this morning I am the only smartly dressed person on the entire campsite.

Around 8.45 a.m. I set off, heading straight for the PC and printer manufacturer, arriving there shortly after 9 a.m., parked the car, and walked to the entrance to the company premises. I know from experience how difficult it is to get past a security guard without an invitation letter. I've already tried that in Britain and Germany, sometimes with success, sometimes without. This is now the first time in France. How will the porter react? Will he let me pass? Let's find out.

I am nervous. My French isn't nearly as good as my English. I pull myself together, produce my best French, and ask the porter if it might be possible to speak to an HR manager. "Would you like to apply for a job?" he asks. "Yes, that's exactly what I would like to do. I'm from Germany, lived in the UK for a few years, and would now like to work in France." The porter thinks for a moment and then says I should go into the entrance hall, as the lady at reception could provide more information.

Then I'm actually past the porter, standing on the company

premises, and marching in the direction of the entrance hall. I still cannot believe it! Sometimes you are just lucky. My excitement increases. Maybe there is a real chance here.

I enter the entrance hall. The interior design is still being worked on, and everything is brand new. At the reception, I briefly explained my request. The receptionist doesn't seem surprised at all. "Yes, we are looking for staff", she replies. "The new plant in Grenoble will open soon and the colleagues in the HR department interview applicants every day." However, everyone is busy at the moment, and I have to ring them up. She writes a name and a phone number on a piece of paper and hands it over to me. Unfortunately, I cannot call from reception and would have to do so from a public telephone box. However, I know from experience that a phone call will not do much as I will simply be told to apply in writing. If I want to achieve something straight away, I would have to introduce myself in person. That's the only way I'd have the chance to explain on the spot why I'm here and what I'm planning to do.

I leave the entrance hall and walk back towards the main gate. If I leave the company premises now and the phone call is unsuccessful, I will certainly not be able to get back inside again. Right now, I'm still within the company premises. However, once I leave again, then there is nothing more I can do.

Near the gate, I spontaneously decide to stay inside and look for the HR department myself. I have nothing to lose, stop, turn around, and walk back to the office building. However, I cannot walk through the entrance hall again because the receptionist will recognise me and I thus sneak along the outside wall of the brand-new office building as inconspicuously as possible. In the process, I check every door to see if it can be opened. Unfortunately, all entrances are locked. However, endurance and persistence are often rewarded, as they are today. At the very end of the building complex, there is a door that is not locked. This is the opportunity!

I enter and find myself in a long corridor. Cables are lying around everywhere, and the rooms are empty, as some of them are still under construction. I walk down the corridor, opening doors, looking for HR, but have not the slightest idea where it might be. The plant consists of four large building complexes. I'm currently in the rearmost part and meet some busy workers. Nobody takes any notice of me.

Suddenly, completely unexpectedly, a uniformed security guard stands in front of me. What now? In such a case, one must not show any fear and appear self-confident. I greet him. He looks at me in astonishment and asks: "What are you doing here?" I briefly describe the situation. Attack is the best defence. How will he react?

Being German seems to have a positive effect on the man. His brother, he notes, lives in Frankfurt/Main. He visits him once a year and says he likes Germany. This is of course extremely positive for me. Could I succeed in leveraging his sympathy for my native country? I let him rave about Germany for a while and then asked specifically for directions to the HR department. To my great surprise, he thinks about how he could help me. To stay on the company premises, I would need a visitor's pass, he then says. Without such authorization, I should not be here at all. While I am still thinking about how to proceed, the kind security guard actually gives me a temporary visitor's pass. This means that I can now move around the company premises completely legally. The friendly man even describes the way to the HR office - which in this case means that he at least tries - because he doesn't know the new buildings that well either. "Just walk along this corridor and you will reach the entrance hall. Ask there at the reception, they will give you more detailed information." However, this is rather inconvenient because I would like to avoid seeing the receptionist again. She would recognise me, wonder why I'm still here, and point to the phone number she gave me earlier.

I walk along the corridor, there's no other way. Only a few yards separate me from the entrance hall when I discover a staircase to my right. Now I have a choice. Either I go straight into the entrance hall, where I am sure I'll be recognised and won't get any further. Or I use these stairs and continue to search for the HR department on my own.

The decision is not difficult. I turn right, climb the stairs, open a few doors, and soon find myself in an open-plan office. Employees are sitting at desks as this office space is already furnished. I have finally come to the right place and I ask the staff member closest to me for the contact person whose name I was given earlier at reception. The young lady wants to know whether I want to apply for a job. "Yes, that's exactly what I intend to do", I reply. She leads me to a table and asks me to fill in a form. After that was done, she told me that I would be informed in writing should I be invited for an interview. However, I cannot wait that long. I explained to her that I would only be in Grenoble for a few days and, for this reason, a job interview would have to take place at short notice. She looks at me a little helplessly but then asks me to follow her, leads me to a lady whose desk is already stacked with application papers and explains, that this lady is responsible for scheduling interviews. The woman skims my CV and seems interested. However, accommodating another appointment at short notice in a fairly busy schedule could be problematic and since she needs some time, she asked me to call her this afternoon, as maybe she could tell me more then. I have to accept this as I really cannot get any further at this point. However, I am very happy with what I have just achieved.

Back in the car, I pick up the list of companies and continue with the job search. I'm highly motivated, and full of self-confidence after this partial success. This positive feeling is very helpful now.

I reach the next company, park the car, and walk to the main gate but cannot get past the porter. No appointment, no entry. The security guard strictly follows the rules.

Fortunately, there are more companies.

At the entrance to the next one, no porter blocks my way and the administration building can be reached directly from the street. I enter, the receptionist calls the HR department and hands me the phone. The lady at the other end of the line is rather surprised and it seems as if it does not happen every day that someone tries to get a job using such a direct approach, especially not a foreigner. However, only the HR manager can decide, and he's on vacation. As far as she knows, there are currently no vacancies in the export department. However, I am welcome to apply in writing. Thus, I cannot get any further here but it nevertheless was an attempt and every possibility, however remote, is worth exploring.

The next company is just around the corner. New place, a new chance. I am back to the days of my job hunt in the UK. This particular company manufactures construction machines. Unfortunately, another security guard blocks the entrance. Even though I have little hope of getting past him, I don't back down and try, and am permitted to pass. I have to wait a few minutes in the visitor's room next to the gatehouse before an employee from HR appears. I briefly describe my previous career and the man is impressed. "Unfortunately you come at a very unfavourable time", he says. There is currently a strict hiring freeze throughout the entire company. Unfortunately, even if he wanted to, he couldn't do anything for me at the moment. However, he keeps my CV, wishes me all the best, and provides some helpful information about local businesses.

It's noon, and I take a break before continuing with my job search.

At around 2 p.m., I am in front of the guardhouse of another potential opportunity. To my surprise, I am allowed to pass. The porter gives me a permit and provides directions to the personnel office, and I am already on the company premises. I find the office, have to wait for a moment, am greeted by a secretary, deliver a copy of my CV, and outline my request. Again I have to wait a few minutes, and then she returns and explains that I can talk to someone responsible for exports. Everything runs perfectly. I was able to pass through the gate without any problems and was even allowed to visit the export department. If that isn't a success!

I am fetched and taken to the office of the export manager. However, he seems to have very little time, the phone keeps ringing and frequently interrupts our conversation. That's not exactly ideal. "Are you a mechanical engineer?" he wants to know. "Unfortunately not, I studied industrial management", I reply. "Regrettably, there are currently no vacancies in this field", he informs me. He also seems interested in my language skills. However, he cannot do more at the moment than copy my certificates and keep the duplicates. If I were a mechanical engineer, who knows, I might have been successful here. Nevertheless, this interview was a personal success, since it took place without a written application or invitation.

At 3 p.m., it is time to call the HR department of the PC and printer manufacturer I visited this morning. To my surprise, there is excellent news! I'm supposed to appear tomorrow at 9.30 a.m. for a first official job interview. Does that suit me? Of course it does! Awesome! I cannot quite believe it yet. What a success!

With this phone call, all hopes I had been nourishing could have been burst. Sometimes joy and disappointment are so close together. That is another proof that one should never give up.

There are two more companies on my schedule for today.

One of them manufactures photocopying machines. The administration building with its glazed frontage and a modern fountain in front of the main entrance is impressive. However, before I can reach the entrance, a security guard stops me. I try to persuade him to let me through but have no success. At least he gives me a phone number and a contact person. I should call there.

Hence, I go back to the public telephone box. Luckily I still have enough change. A woman's voice answers. I presented my request and asked if I could hand in my application documents in person. The woman is not even slightly surprised and tells me to drop by.

I go back to the security guard and this time the gate opens and I am allowed to pass. Actually, I have no proof that I really called and was invited. As persistent as the man was earlier, he now believes me thoughtlessly and lets me pass. I cannot suppress a slight victorious grin as I walk past him. At reception, I mention the name of the person I just spoke to and a lady fetches me a few minutes later. However, she's in a hurry, takes my documents and promises to check them. Should the company be interested I would be notified. That's it. In the end, I wasn't very successful, apart from the fact that I got past an extremely persistent security guard.

It is now past 4 p.m. I still want to visit another company today but have to hurry, otherwise, all employees will have gone home. I received the tip to visit this company today from one of my interlocutors.

Finding the company is not that easy. I get lost several times but finally reach the location.

It's almost 5 p.m. now, maybe too late for what I intend to do. Nevertheless, I give it a try.

Here, too, a porter watches over the gate. However, the young man is very helpful and calls the HR department. Someone is still there, and I could have a face-to-face interview. The porter describes the way and I'm on the factory premises. An employee is waiting for me, but is in a hurry, as closing time is approaching. The timing is unfavourable. I hand over my application documents. They will be checked and I will be informed.

That was the last visit for today. An exhausting, adventurous and, on the whole, very successful day lies behind me. I return to the campsite. On the way there, I quickly buy some food for tonight.

That evening, I lie down on the air mattress next to the tent, daydream in the evening sun, and imagine how amazing it would be to be able to live and work in this beautiful area. However, I am not that far yet. Despite all the daydreaming, I shouldn't lose sight of reality. There's a hard task ahead of me tomorrow. I was invited for an interview, but I am sure nothing will be given to me. If I want the job, I have to convince the person in charge. I should be rested for this. Hence, I slip into my sleeping bag to be fit for tomorrow.

Wednesday, May 3rd. I get up early, shower, get dressed, and leave the campsite at almost exactly 9 a.m. Twenty minutes later, I reach the company where I have the appointment at 9.30 a.m. This time, I am officially invited, pass the porter without any problems, enter the main building, and have to wait a moment before I am fetched by the lady with whom I made the appointment. She also conducts the interview. She informs me that the corporate language is English and we thus communicate in this language. That suits me well because I feel much more confident in English than in French.

The conversation lasted almost an hour. The lady informs me about the company and then describes the position for which a suitable employee is being sought. They are looking for a "Customer Support Engineer" who maintains contact between the plants in Europe and the USA. Very good English language skills are required. No problem for me. German language skills are not specifically required, however, would be an advantage. Then I describe my previous professional career. Finally, she wants to know whether my wife would also like to live in Grenoble. "Of course she would. France is her native country and the landscape is beautiful."

After about an hour, this first job interview comes to an end. My interlocutor will talk to the people in charge of the relevant department during the next few days. If there is a second appointment, I will be notified within the next two weeks.

I am satisfied, as I was able to attend a job interview today with a company that has a very interesting position to fill. The trip to Grenoble has already paid off. I found this unique opportunity by chance, certainly also through luck, but above all through my initiative. I would really like to work for this international company. However, my application must still be processed and now it is just a matter of waiting and hoping that there will be a second interview.

After leaving the company premises, I want to take a closer look at the city centre of Grenoble before I return home tomorrow. Who knows, maybe I will get the job and this place will become our new home. I stroll through the city centre, buy a fresh baguette and some cheese, sit down on a park bench, and enjoy the relaxing feeling of pride and contentment. On the way back to the campsite, I buy a bottle of red wine, because, on this last evening, I want to celebrate. All in all, the trip to Grenoble was much more successful than expected.

I open the bottle of wine, eat the rest of the bread and cheese, am happy, and feel free. After dinner, I sit down in front of the tent and admire the last rays of the evening sun, which make the peaks of the surrounding mountains shine in a matt pink. Breathtakingly beautiful! Then it gets dark. The sky is clear, and the first stars appear. I could sit and look into the night sky for hours if it wasn't becoming so chilly. The cold drives me into the tent and the warm sleeping bag.

Back home, I have to wait and see whether I will be invited for a second interview or not.

The following week, I took part in two job interviews in Germany.

On Friday, May 12th, the phone rings at around 9 a.m. The call comes from Grenoble. I am invited for a second interview on Wednesday, May 24th.

After I put the phone down, I have to pinch myself to be sure that I am not dreaming. I am overwhelmed by a feeling of immense joy! It may be possible to live and work in this beautiful city in the mountains. However, before this happens there is still a lot of work to do. The second interview will certainly not be easy. This time I have to convince the relevant department that I am the right person for the job.

A few days later, I received a phone call from a company in Munich that invited me for an interview that is also scheduled for May 24th. Thus, I have to make a decision because I cannot visit both companies on the same day. I choose Grenoble and try to move the invitation from Munich to another date. However, this only works to a limited extent, since my interview partner is going on holiday after the suggested date. This is risky! Maybe I will not be invited again after that. However, under no circumstances am I postponing Grenoble.

On Tuesday, May 23rd, I am on my way to the French Alps again. This time by train at the expense of the company that invites me.

I reach Geneva via Frankfurt, Basel, and Bern. There, I use the two-hour stopover for a walk by the lake, reach Grenoble at 9 p.m., and take a taxi to the hotel where a room has already been booked. What a difference compared to my first arrival in this city just three weeks ago. I do not have to worry about anything tonight. A comfortable room in a luxurious hotel is the reward for courage and persistence.

I go to bed early because tomorrow I have a very important day ahead of me.

Wednesday, May 24th. Bright sunshine in the morning. I convince myself that nothing can go wrong on such a glorious day, have breakfast, and then rest a bit because my appointment is only at 1.30 p.m.

I arrive on time at the reception of the PC and printer manufacturer, where I am hoping for the breakthrough today. A management consultant picks me up. She leads the first part of the interview which consists of four separate parts. Each of these four parts lasts precisely one hour. The interlocutors change every time, while the questions are largely the same. There are almost no breaks in between the sessions. The management consultant communicates in French. Even though I do not feel as confident in this language as I do in English, I am doing well.

My second interview partner is the group leader to whom the

new employee will report. This time we speak English which suits me very well.

The third interlocutor is the head of the department, to whom the group leader reports. Again, we speak English. From him, I learn more about the vacant position. The most important language within the company is English. However, the successful applicant must also be fluent in French to be able to pass on information to their French colleagues. He wants to know how well I speak French. "Unfortunately, my French is currently not as fluent as my English", I reply. "However, once I'm in the country, I will most certainly improve my language skills." This question was prompted due to the current situation the company faces of another employee with English as their mother tongue who still has problems with the French language, although he has lived in France for quite some time.

The fourth and final interview partner is the marketing manager. And again, there is no break. I am tired, and not as focussed as I was at the beginning, and that is always dangerous! He leaves it up to me whether to conduct the interview in English or French. I choose English.

After four hours, the interview is finally over and a taxi takes me back to the hotel where I rest a bit and then go for an evening walk. From now on, I can only wait until I receive the outcome of today's conversation during the next week. I know that I am not the only applicant for this position and that several other applicants were invited to the second round of interviews. However, being one of them is already a huge achievement.

The next morning, a train takes me back home via Geneva and Basel.

Friday, June 2nd. Still no reply from Grenoble. I want to know the result, and thus I ring them up and ask about the current status.

Unfortunately, the answer is negative. I will receive a written notification within the next week. The dream of living and working in the French Alps comes to a sudden end in just a few seconds.

I should have chosen French for the fourth and final interview session, instead of English. That was a small but probably crucial mistake.

One is always wiser in hindsight. While it was a great opportunity there could be only one winner and this time, it wasn't me. However, my chance will also definitely come, I just have to keep on searching courageously.

Regarding my motivation, I am prepared. In case of a cancellation, I made up my mind to travel to France a second time to search for a job in Orléans. Instead of being disappointed, I immediately start planning another adventure.

The thought of this new challenge quickly makes me forget the defeat.

On Tuesday, June 6th, I set off and reached Saarbrücken on the French border in the early afternoon. I used to study here and graduated from the Technical College and the University of the Saarland in 1982/83. I have not been here for years, and memories resurface.

I wanted to drive past Saarbrücken to get as close as possible to Orléans today. However, without hesitation, I change my original plan, leave the motorway, drive to the city centre, and immerse myself in memories. It is nice to be here again. Everything is still familiar. The memory of my successful study period strengthens my self-confidence.

At around 5 p.m., I cross the French border. The motorway stretches west towards Paris. Even though I won't reach Orléans today, I intend to drive as far as possible. That evening, I am within eighty kilometres of Paris.

Around 11 p.m. I can hardly keep my eyes open, stop at the next service station, park the car between trucks, whose drivers are also staying here overnight, fold down the seat and try to get some rest. Actually, I just want to relax for a moment and then drive on. However, I soon fall asleep.

When I wake up, it is already 7 a.m. and I continue my journey.

Near the centre of Paris, I get stuck in a traffic jam and decide to leave the motorway to bypass the French capital on country roads. This gets me out of the traffic jam, but not to my destination as orientation is difficult without a detailed map. I drive in circles, return to the spot where I left the motorway, and join it again. Fortunately, the commuter traffic has slowed down and I am making good progress now. I am really glad to have finally bypassed the big city. The further I get away from Paris, the emptier the motorway becomes.

I reach Orléans around 1 p.m. In contrast to Grenoble, I know this city well, and pitch my tent at a campsite at the Loire river. Now it is time to rest. After a short recovery break, I intend to visit the Chamber of Commerce and Industry to get an address list of local companies. Just like in Grenoble, I plan to draw up a sort of ranking list of companies located in Orléans.

I set out on foot and asked my way around. It doesn't take long before I am standing in front of the Chamber of Commerce. There, I present my request, receive the list, make a selection, mark the addresses of companies that seem interesting to me, and locate them on the city map. I would like to visit all of these companies over the next few days to explore job opportunities. My motivation could hardly be better.

In the evening, I stroll contentedly along the Loire. It is a mild summer evening, and there is no room for negative thoughts.

On Thursday, June 8th, I start job hunting. Will I be as successful in Orléans as I was in Grenoble? First, I plan to visit an international IT company.

The company in question has several locations, and I drive to the nearest one. At the entrance, a security guard stops me. I learned that the HR department is at another location, a few kilometres from here. When I get there, I stand in front of a high fence. There are trees behind the boundary, and no buildings can be seen. They are certainly hidden among the trees and not visible from the outside. Due to the tough competition between leading companies, none of them wants to reveal too much about themselves. This probably explains this hidden location. I drive along the fence. There has to be an entrance somewhere. Behind a locked gate, a road leads into the forest. I spot a gatehouse on the premises. One can talk to the security guards via an interphone. I have no other choice but to use this facility and push the button. A brisk voice asks what I want. "I would like to talk to someone from HR", I reply. "Do you have an appointment?" "No, unfortunately not." That's it, I cannot get any further. Successfully persuading security guards to gain entry to a premises via an interphone is virtually impossible. I should apply in writing and if the company is interested, I will receive an invitation to an interview. Getting through is impossible for the time being. I am disappointed. I had high hopes regarding this company, especially since I was fairly successful at a competitor in Grenoble.

After this first attempt, I pass the administration building of a well-known perfume manufacturer. New opportunity, new attempt. A porter is overseeing the premises and at least I can persuade him to give me the name and phone number of an employee in the HR department.

I continue my job hunt in the city centre. An impressive administration building arouses my interest. The name of the company is not visible, but it does not cost anything to ask. The porter at the entrance displays a completely different behaviour. "Of course you can visit the HR department", he says and even tells me how to get there. It all happens so quickly that I am astonished at how easily I can pass through. There are porters whom one cannot get past at all, and there are gates that open all by themselves. One such gate just opened up in front of me. I quickly slip through before it can close again. At the reception, I learned that this is the head office of a bank. The receptionist is friendly but also puzzled that someone appears unannounced and enquires about employment. Nevertheless, she calls HR and says that someone will come to talk to me. I wait a moment, and then a lady appears. She is also friendly, and I explain the reason for my visit. Unfortunately, no knowledge of foreign languages would be needed, but occasionally employees with experience in the banking business. Regrettably, I cannot help with that. Nevertheless, this first conversation was the first partial success of today.

Next, I called the HR department of the perfume company whose porter wouldn't let me through earlier. Although the site is only a five-minute drive away, I am unable to arrange a meeting.

To save myself from making further trips in vain, I call a few more companies from the public telephone box. However, I cannot arrange any meetings.

By now, it is already afternoon and I intend to explore two more industrial estates in the north of the city. There, I discovered a few companies that could be worth a visit tomorrow.

In the evening, I am quite pleased with what I have achieved today. Even though I have not been able to find a job yet, I got by well using the French language. I put that under personal experience. The more companies I visit in France, the more confident I become in the foreign language, and the more courageously I use it.

That night, I slept very well in my tent on the banks of the Loire.

The next morning the sun is shining, the Loire is flowing calmly, what a relaxing, peaceful sight. I cannot wait to go out and continue my job search.

Friday, June 9th. I am heading for one of the two industrial estates I spotted yesterday afternoon. There, I notice a company with numerous flags of different countries in front of the entrance. A company that displays flags might also be interested in employees with foreign language skills.

The gate to the company premises is open, and no porter is in sight. I presented my request at reception and managed to secure an appointment for an interview with the HR manager right away. What a positive start! I learned that a technical product is manufactured here and that they are interested in foreign language skills, but unfortunately, the export share of their total turnover is currently still very low. However, there are plans to expand the business activities during the coming years. This means that the HR manager cannot do anything for me at the moment but in a few years, people like me will be needed. The conversation was very informative and provided the first sense of achievement of the day.

I visit several medium-sized companies, unfortunately with little success. At some of them, I can hand in my documents, while at others I cannot even get past the porter.

A small engineering company offered me a job as a casual worker, comparable to the first jobs I had in Britain. However, I am not interested in casual employment. If I were a few years younger, I might start all over again the way I did four years ago. But now I am thirty-three years old, have to support a family, and need a qualified job. Nevertheless, I am happy about this partial success, even though I cannot use it.

At another company, I managed to enter the company premises in a rather unique way. When I arrive, the gate is closed and I am just about to continue when a vehicle approaches. The gate opens automatically and also gives me the opportunity to enter the company premises, especially since there is neither a porter nor a camera nearby. I quickly make up my mind to take advantage of this unexpected opportunity. As I walk through the gate, I assume the driver of the vehicle will stop and tell me that I am not supposed to be there. But nothing happens. The car drives past me and the driver pays no attention to me at all. As I head for the entrance of an office building, the gate closes behind me. At the reception, my appearance causes some astonishment. After the initial surprise, I was informed that the HR manager was currently out of the office. I hand over my documents to a secretary, which is all I can do.

I take a break, eat something, and visit other companies during the afternoon. However, there is no success like in Grenoble.

In the evening, all the companies on my list were visited. Although I couldn't find a job, I actively communicated in French and thereby strengthened my self-confidence. Hence, my trip to Orléans was not in vain.

If one wants to achieve something, one must be fully committed. Naturally, one also needs a bit of luck to meet the right person in the right place at the right time. However, only those who search intensively and are not discouraged by challenges and defeats have at least the chance to come across one of these lucky moments. I was fortunate a couple of times while searching for jobs in the UK and took advantage of it. The failure when returning to Germany was painful. For a short period, my confidence suffered. However, I picked myself up and tried again. In Grenoble, I was almost successful and if I hadn't been actively looking for a job there, I would never have come across this opportunity.

Nothing was in vain. Unfortunately, there was no success in Orléans, but it could have been.

I am tired. All the walking, talking, explaining, and persuading takes its toll. That evening, I sit in front of my tent that is pitched overlooking the Loire that flows calmly past me, surrounded by bushes and trees that are beginning to shine intensely in the mild evening sun. The tranquillity of the landscape has a calming effect.

I think about the return trip, which will again lead through the Saarland, and spontaneously decide to explore job opportunities there as well.

Saturday, June 10th. I set out late in the morning.

Near Verdun, I pass the former battlefields of the First World War. At that time, it was not as easy to get from the Meuse to the Moselle as it is today. I pass the front line of the battles that took place back then. Today, one can pass this line without any problems.

I stop somewhere amid the landscape, take a short break, and look back towards Verdun. Dark storm clouds are gathering on the western horizon, thunder is rumbling in the distance. This is roughly how people must have heard the thunder of the super-heavy artillery guns during the war. Fortunately, today it is just a thunderstorm. Again, it rumbles in the distance.

I drive on, reach Saarbrücken, head for a campsite, and pitch the tent before it gets too dark. On Sunday, I spend the day in my former student town and reminisce about this period of my life.

On Monday, June 12th, my job search in the Saarland starts at the job centre. However, with little success. Unfortunately, there is nothing they can do. Since my main place of residence is in another city, the job centre there is responsible.

Why am I relying on others again? If I want to achieve something during the next few days, I have to be proactive.

I visited the Chamber of Commerce and Industry and received a list of all the companies in the Saarland that export a great deal of their goods. Anyone who exports also requires employees with foreign language skills. And this is where I have something to offer. I retreat into a quiet corner, work out a plan, and start job hunting.

The very first attempt ends at the gatehouse. No appointment, no entrance.

Next, I try my luck at a manufacturer of ceramics. Around 12.30 p.m., I reach the company headquarters. Parts of the buildings are being renovated, craftsmen are walking around, and the gate is open. According to my motto: "Where a door is open, go in and try your luck", I enter the administration building. After a few meters, a security guard stops me. Is this the end now? Luckily not yet. When I ask about HR, the man leads me to a room for visitors from where I can call the HR department. An employee on the other end of the line informs me that the HR manager is currently out of the office but will be back around 2 p.m. I should come back then and will be able to talk to him.

After the lunch break, I am back on time. At the main entrance, I pass the porter without any problems, since I have an official appointment. I am asked to wait a moment, and then the HR manager has time to see me. I describe my situation as well as my previous career and studies. He listens with interest, keeps my documents, and asks me to submit a written application. During the next few days, he will clarify internally whether there are currently any vacancies for which I would be suitable. This is not yet a job offer, but at least the HR manager is interested in what I have to offer.

On the way back to Saarbrücken, I want to visit a company

that I know from my student days. It is almost the end of the day and I have to hurry up. I reach the company premises, enter the administration building, knock on a few doors, and open them but no one is there. Strange! I climb a flight of stairs and try my luck on the first floor. Finally, a lady crosses my path. I ask about the HR department. "You are lucky, the HR manager is still here", she says and leads me to his office, but no one is there either. I was told that I should wait as he would come back soon. I sit down on a chair in front of the desk and wait. It doesn't take long before the man appears. We have an interesting conversation. Unfortunately, he cannot promise me anything specific in the short term, as my application has to be discussed internally first. He keeps my documents and asks me to hand in a letter of application.

There is hope at two companies I visited today and it had a positive effect that I went by in person.

Now it is already 5 p.m., and too late to visit other companies. I return to the campsite, study the local newspaper, and discover an interesting job advert. An employee is wanted in the export department. As the company in question is not far away, I have decided to visit them tomorrow.

Tuesday, June 13th. After breakfast, I am on my way again. I expect a great deal from today's visit because according to the job advertisement, there is a vacancy for which I meet the requirements.

The porter stops me at the entrance. I show him the advertisement, and he calls HR. After this, I am allowed to pass through and hand in my documents personally. Now I just have to get an interview. Since I am already there and do not have to travel from far away, it would certainly be cheaper for both parties to have an initial interview today. While this is a logical proposal, the attempt fails and I can only submit my documents. The selection process would then take its usual course. I am disappointed, as I would have liked to know more about the advertised position and especially to make a personal impression. However, I will be notified in a few weeks.

I returned to the campsite without the success I had hoped for and no longer had a great desire to visit other companies. Based on the list of the Chamber of Industry and Commerce, I will contact interesting companies in writing next week. I dismantle the tent and start my return journey. Almost three hundred and forty kilometres lie ahead of me.

Altogether, I was away for a week, covered around two thousand kilometres, and visited numerous companies in France and some in the Saarland. Apart from disappointments, there were also rather respectable partial successes. On the whole, I am quite satisfied. I took action, improved my French language skills, gained precious experience, strengthened my self-confidence, and achieved partial success. Even though this time I am not returning with as much success as I did from Grenoble, this does not matter because if you don't try, you cannot win either.

Back home, I am very happy to see my little family again. It is amazing how an almost eleven-month-old child changes in just one week. Had I left my wife and child in the UK earlier this year and gone ahead alone to explore the professional situation, I would have missed out on a great deal of Rebecca's development. This is why we took a great risk, stayed together, gave up our residence in the UK and therefore, unfortunately, have to overcome a defeat. However, now is not the time to look back to identify culprits. We should look ahead, keep trying, and make the best of the current situation.

I select export-oriented companies from the lists of the

Chambers of Industry and Commerce and send letters of application to German and French companies.

Shortly thereafter, I was invited to an interview by a local company that is looking for an employee to intensify their export planning. The interview is constructive, and the company representative says they will get back to me.

In early July, Debby and Andrew, our Australian friends from Cambridge, visit us for a long weekend. They now live in Switzerland. It is the first time we have met friends from the UK since we left and there is a lot to tell.

More invitations for interviews arrive.

The local company that wants to intensify their export planning invites me for the second interview during which I meet the export- and sales manager and receive a detailed description of the area of responsibility. After this meeting, I am very confident.

Then, I attend an interview near Koblenz.

Shortly thereafter, I finally managed to break through. The company with which I have already had two interviews regarding export planning offered me a job contract. My employment would start on August 1st.

SUCCESS: EMPLOYMENT CONTRACT IN GERMANY

On Friday, July 14th, there are still some details to be clarified regarding the new employment contract. This time, I am much more careful than I was at the beginning of the year. I talk to the export manager in detail and am introduced to my new colleagues, see the workplace, and get a detailed overview of what to expect. The job and the salary meet my expectations.

Success at last! I sign the new contract.

Surprisingly, I am now receiving many invitations to further job interviews. One company even wants to talk to me in the UK. What am I going to do with all the invitations that continue to arrive? Do I let them expire, like at the end of last year after signing my previous contract? Or do I visit all of these companies to find out whether there might be a more lucrative job on offer? I decided to attend all interviews that take place before the first of August. This time, I want to find the best job.

On Monday, July 17th, I attended an interview for the first time, knowing that I already have an employment contract. Will I be as convincing as if I had no job yet? Will my interlocutors notice anything? This is a completely new approach. However, this is exactly what is interesting. One has to try everything once. The experiment succeeds. I appear confident, and my interlocutor does not notice anything. The company will get back to me in a few weeks. However, this will not put me in a difficult position to make a decision because the job on offer is by far not as interesting as the one I already have.

The next day, I visited the manufacturer of ceramics in the Saarland where I was able to secure a first appointment a few weeks ago through my own initiative. I got a second appointment, this time with the head of the overseas department. However, unfortunately, nothing can be resolved today.

With a heavy heart, I decide to cancel the invitation for an interview in Britain. Even though I really would have liked to participate in this interview, we've decided to return to the Continent. With the responsibility for a child, safety comes before adventure.

On Friday, there are two job interviews in the Stuttgart area. The manufacturer of measuring machines, where I tried unsuccessfully to make a spontaneous appearance a few weeks ago, invited me for a meeting in the morning.

In the afternoon, the German branch of a British company would like to get to know me as well. Since the two locations are very close to each other, it should be possible to visit both companies on the same day. However, the conversation with the manager of the measuring machine manufacturer is extremely interesting and I thus do not risk interrupting it. In the end, there is unfortunately not enough time for the second appointment.

More interviews follow and I also travel to the Saarland again. The company in response to whose newspaper advert I submitted my certificates, would now like to get to know me personally.

During the last three weeks, I received twelve invitations for interviews. I was able to attend ten of them, while two had to be cancelled due to scheduling reasons.

We spend the last days of July in France and celebrate Rebecca's first birthday with the family. Marie is staying there together with Rebecca for another week, while I am returning to Germany to start my new job on August 1st.

At work, I get to know my colleagues and the new products. Every day work begins.

On one weekend in August, we visit Nancy and Wilfried, our friends from Belper, in the Bavarian Alps, where they are currently on vacation. After the excitement of the past few months, our daily routine is slowly beginning to return to normal. We spend relaxing days in the mountains and have a lot to tell each other. Naturally, we are very curious to get the latest news from our former adopted country. As we sit together and chat, it is almost like we are back in Derbyshire for a while.

In mid-September, I attend the industrial fair in Hanover, which presents the ideal opportunity to get to know the new products, meet customers, and study the competition. I may even meet some of my former British colleagues who will most likely be attending this trade fair as well.

Then a huge surprise awaits me! My former British employer's booth is located directly opposite ours. The two booths could not have been closer together. What a coincidence at this vast exhibition centre.

Here I am at my new employer's booth and look back into the past. Everything is still so familiar over there, the people, the product, the language. Naturally, there is a happy reunion and I have to answer numerous questions concerning how I am doing, where I live now, how my wife and little daughter are doing, whether I miss the UK, and so on.

I also found out that my previous position is still vacant and my former boss wants to know whether I would like to return. Deep in my heart, I would still love to do that. However, not only my interests are decisive, but also those of my family. Hence there is no returning to the UK, no matter how tempting the thought might be.

The time at the trade fair is very interesting. I get to know my new colleagues better, familiarise myself with the new products, and have technical details explained to me.

A few times, however, I catch myself lost in thought looking at the booth of my previous employer and remembering the past. I worked for this British company for three years, and everything is still familiar. However, there is no way back. I have made my decision and I must not get sentimental now. However, knowing that I could get my previous job in the UK back feels very good.

RENTING A FLAT
AND SETTLING DOWN
IN GERMANY

We start looking for a flat in mid-October which once again proves to be difficult. We thought that there was only a housing shortage in and around large cities but found out that things do not look much better in smaller towns either.

We try to find accommodation through real estate agents, but the results are quite frustrating. At the moment, nothing suitable is on offer. Adverts for accommodation in the newspaper are also sparse. Luckily we are not pressed for time. However, after nine months, we would like to finally live in our own flat again.

It takes a few weeks until we receive an offer and we like the flat right away. Hence, it is important to make a quick decision. Our lucky streak seems to be returning. The flat is located in a pleasant residential area, it is spacious with three rooms, and the kitchen is fully equipped.

We move in on Thursday, November 2nd. Now we finally have a home of our own again.

During the following weeks, we are busy unpacking cardboard boxes and crates, and assembling and setting up furniture. Slowly but surely, things become more comfortable and we're settled again.

At the end of November, my four-month probation period comes to an end and I am accepted into permanent employment. Our lives are beginning to normalize.

This year was extremely eventful. But now, we've made it and gained a foothold in Germany which was not that easy. It took almost one year until we settled down again. When I moved to the UK, it also took almost one year before I found a qualified job. Everything needs time.

When the traditional New Year's Eve fireworks light up the night sky at midnight on December 31st, I feel relieved. The year is over. It was unexpectedly turbulent, and exciting, and had various ups and downs. Our foreign adventure that began on March 11, 1985, with my arrival in Harwich has a happy ending today on December 31, 1989.

The fireworks subside, and only a few rockets rise into the dark sky. Our little daughter sleeps deeply, and she doesn't even notice the hustle and bustle. A new year lies ahead of us and as always we ask ourselves the question: What will happen to us in the future? But we look ahead with a lot of confidence. We've returned to the Continent, integrated, and gained a foothold in Germany again. What lies ahead of us now is another adventure on our journey through life.

In the early minutes of 1990, as so often, my thoughts returned to the UK. These four years were something very special, and I will always remember them.

EPILOGUE

We've risked a lot, and even though we were largely successful, we also had to cope with various challenges and setbacks.

Although we would do many things the same way again, in hindsight, we would perhaps approach some things differently. Despite intensive planning, I made a serious mistake when returning to Germany as I should not have changed jobs and my place of residence at the same time. It is always better to be careful.

The decision to go abroad for a few years to gain work and life experience and to improve my language skills was right. I would make the same decision again.

Our time in Britain turned out to be much more successful than we had hoped. We were definitely very lucky. However, if we hadn't risked anything, we would never have had this luck.

The terminations of the first temporary jobs were risky, but this turned out to be the right decision. Despite the high unemployment rate, especially for unskilled workers, I took the risk and gradually improved my professional situation. Courage and persistence paid off.

Prolonging our stay in the UK from two to four years can be judged differently. After two years in the English-speaking world, a few years in France would have been an interesting option regarding another foreign language. However, in 1987 we had just managed to secure permanent employment contracts in addition to relatively good salaries that allowed us to afford two cars and a house in the countryside. We did not want to give that up to start all over again in another country.

The decision to return to Germany was right for us in the long term. It was well prepared but turned out to be unexpectedly complicated.

On the whole, we are successful again even though it took some time and didn't proceed quite as smoothly as expected. However, due to a positive attitude, good education, special knowledge, and a great deal of initiative, we made it relatively quickly.

Our friends in the UK played an important role in the success of our foreign adventure. They always made us feel safe. Whenever we needed help, they were there. Especially during the crucial first year, they gave us the necessary support that we so desperately needed. The certainty of always being able to rely on someone gave us the necessary confidence and strength we needed to be successful.

Those who can afford to do so should live and work in another country for a certain period. The experiences gained abroad do not only expand one's horizons, but one also learns another language, and other mindsets and approaches. However, it is important to never get discouraged. Every new day holds new opportunities. What remains forever are priceless memories of an exciting period of life, a time of unlimited freedom in which one could take one's fate into one's own hands and determine the direction one wants their life to take. All this provides enormous strength for future challenges.

ABOUT THE AUTHOR

Johannes M. Ludwig (born in 1956 in Southern Germany) studied business economics at the Technical College and the University of the Saarland (Western Germany) and gained his first professional experience as a sales representative in Northern Germany.

In 1985 he decided, together with his French wife, to move to the UK for a few years. The couple chose Derby as their place of residence, Osnabrück's twin town in England.

After returning to Germany, Ludwig worked for an international group of companies until his retirement in 2019.

He is married, has two daughters, several grandchildren, and lives in Southern Germany.

He still enjoys returning to the UK, visiting friends, hiking in the picturesque mountains and valleys of Derbyshire, appreciating the sights of the region, and still feels associated with the people and the landscape.